THE REFERENCE SHELF   VOLUME 39 NUMBER 1

FRANCE
UNDER DE GAULLE

EDITED BY
IRWIN ISENBERG

THE H. W. WILSON COMPANY
NEW YORK   1967

THE REFERENCE SHELF

The books in this series contain reprints of articles, excerpts from books, and addresses on current issues and social trends in the United States and other countries. There are six separately bound numbers in each volume, all of which are generally published in the same calendar year. One number is a collection of recent speeches; each of the others is devoted to a single subject and gives background information and discussion from various points of view, concluding with a comprehensive bibliography.

Subscribers to the current volume receive the books as issued. The subscription rate is $12 ($15 foreign) for a volume of six numbers. Single numbers are $3 each.

CONTENTS

I.   INSIDE FRANCE

EDITOR'S INTRODUCTION

Charles de Gaulle, it has often been said, is France. Although this is an obvious oversimplification, it is true that few world leaders command his magnetism, project his sense of grandeur, or possess a style—in words and action—of such eloquence and incisiveness. In these respects, de Gaulle is a unique figure, and his personality and character have been the subject of endless speculation.

It thus seems particularly appropriate to begin this volume with Herbert Lüthy's *Foreign Affairs* essay, an article which is one of the most penetrating to have appeared on de Gaulle in recent years. Professor Lüthy goes back in time to trace the development of key ideas which today form the core of de Gaulle's thought and motivate much of his action.

That de Gaulle is not the sum of France, however, is borne out by the content of the next piece—a sweeping *Current History* article on the quiet, but revolutionary, changes which have occurred throughout the country in the past decade. This article focuses on the immense social transformation which has taken place, on the role of the peasantry and labor in society, and on the place of the arts in French life.

The remaining articles in this section have been selected to offer the reader a survey of some of the more important currents in today's France under de Gaulle. The Headline Series excerpt analyzes and evaluates the governmental structure. "The Once and Future King," taken from *Newsweek,* exposes a little-known side of the French governmental system. A New York *Times* piece then reviews the reasons for the high degree of President de Gaulle's popularity. The *National Review* article presents an unusual viewpoint by speaking of Gaullism's "demise" as a result of the 1965 French presidential elections. This article also speaks of the possibility of a popular front government, with Communist participation, in a post-Gaullist era. The next article presents an alternate view, noting that a coalition of anti-Gaullist forces and Communists is unlikely. The section concludes with a brief look at what French young people are doing and thinking and with a summing up of the de Gaulle years by four prominent Frenchmen.

DE GAULLE: POSE AND POLICY [1]

As long as French foreign policy is nothing else than the personal policy of President de Gaulle, any analysis of it depends essentially on an understanding of his personal psychology. While his psychology is not that of the ordinary political leader, there is nothing impenetrable or mysterious about it. Even the sphinx-like pose which he is fond of assuming is deliberate and calculated; from his earliest writings, he has been consciously creating the ideal portrait of *le grand chef*, who must, as he wrote in 1927, "possess something indefinable, mysterious . . . remain impenetrable to his subordinates, and in this way keep them in suspense." According to a more recent formulation of his, this mystery resides, too, in the political art of "not crystallizing in words that which the future is going to demonstrate," of not defining goals before being assured of their success, and then always appearing to have desired what comes to pass.

This is the ABC of the art of politics. De Gaulle's mastery of *mystère*, which is above all the art of ambiguity and of Pythian formulas, permitted him, when faced with the gravest problem he ever had to meet—the Algerian War—to maneuver among the reefs for four years, to envisage in turn every possible or impossible solution and to see them all miscarry. First there was the offer made to the Algerians to become "whole-share French citizens;" then the mission given the army to "integrate the souls" of the Algerian people; then the grand vision of an African Cali-

[1] From article by Herbert Lüthy, professor of history at the Swiss Federal Institute of Technology, Zürich, Switzerland. *Foreign Affairs.* 43:561-73. Jl. '65. Reprinted by special permission from *Foreign Affairs,* July 1965. Copyright by the Council on Foreign Relations, Inc., New York.

fornia grouping Algeria and French Black Africa in a zone of prosperity around the oil of the Sahara; then the still ambiguous concept of an "Algerian Algeria," independent but associated— all leading finally to the collapse of French colonization in North Africa and the accords of Évian, now hardly more than a scrap of paper. At the end of this tortuous course, the wisdom of the statesman has been "to accept things as they are," to respect the Évian agreements on his side and to accept unflinchingly the violation of them by the other side, in order to show that he is satisfied—and to keep the future open.

The extent of de Gaulle's success in this tragic imbroglio is shown by the fact that the whole world is convinced that from the outset he wanted in his secret heart to end up exactly where he did. This is an improbable hypothesis, and, above all, terribly unjust, for it supposes that de Gaulle willfully deceived and betrayed all those who carried him to power in 1958; but the reputation for being a man of unfathomable cunning does not displease him, and in any case he prefers it to the contrary hypothesis—truer but less grandiose—that, unable to do what he wished, he wished for what he could do. The essential is that the prestige of the leader be preserved; the rest counts for little.

Charles de Gaulle is not a man of mystery. The air of mystery is part of the character which he has created, by calculation as much as by inclination, because it allows him to feint, to maneuver in front of the obstacle and to withdraw, if need be, without losing face. What distinguishes his political style, and what makes him unique, is precisely that he knows how to be an opportunist without appearing to be one, and how to compromise without compromising himself. He believes profoundly in a fate which is stronger than men; and he knows how to take advantage of unforeseen events. His fatalistic side becomes stronger with the wisdom of age: "Regarding the stars, I am imbued with the insignificance of things." But his realism is limited by a number of fundamental ideas, which are unarguable and beyond compromise; they give his policies not only their content but their style. These constants consist of his conception of the world and of politics, the system of coordinates within which his thought evolves, and outside which he refuses to venture: a world of symbols rather than of realities. Before searching in his acts or in his words for hidden designs, we must grasp this basic point; from it all else follows.

The vision of the political world—the *Weltanschauung*—of General de Gaulle is a matter of individual psychology only in so far as his own predestined role in it is concerned. Apart from this crucial detail, it is a vision so imbued with French traditions of the most classic sort that individual psychology plays a lesser part than collective psychology; hence the power of suggestion which his vision holds for Frenchmen. Through de Gaulle a venerable and glorious France takes on the splendor of a spectacular sunset.

II

The biography of Charles de Gaulle (and especially his own version of it) is so well known that we can easily trace the origin of the elements that make up his vision. He was born into an exemplary family in which the father was a teacher of history, literature and classical languages at a Jesuit school in Paris, and in which the cult of France and nostalgia for the legitimate monarchy—*Dieu et le Roi!*—were celebrated with a religious fervor. Reading was in the classics and the lives of heroes: Alexander the Great, Hannibal, Caesar, Joan of Arc, the kings and marshals of France. He grew up among history books in which the world was illumined exclusively by the deeds of France— "nation of heroes and saints"—and among little lead soldiers with which the de Gaulle children reconstructed glorious battles of the past. Like most right-thinking families of the time, the de Gaulles abhorred the Republic and all the regimes which followed 1789, and from childhood Charles learned to make that distinction which for him remains fundamental: the sublime idea of France, predestined leader of the world as soon as she found incarnation in a legitimate sovereign or God-sent hero; and the mass of flesh-and-blood Frenchmen, dedicated to mediocrity, confusion and sterile partisan struggles when lacking the guidance of an anointed leader.

Nothing of the historical imagery and political convictions acquired in childhood was shaken by the years in a Catholic *lycée,* nor, evidently, by his education at the École de Guerre [the War College]. In World War I, the "ambition to serve France" was hardly satisfied by nearly three years of frustration as a prisoner in Germany, during which time he saw continental empires collapse on all sides. In 1927, at the age of 37, the thought of the young Commandant de Gaulle was summed up in a series of lectures given at the École de Guerre, under the presidency of Marshal Pétain, then his idol and patron: "Military Action and the Leader," "On Prestige," "On Character." All were in the heroic and classic style inspired by Plutarch, Caesar and Machiavelli. In them de Gaulle portrayed his ideal of the leader born to command, a vocation to which he clearly felt called.

All this—the naïve faith of childhood and the authoritarian conception of history forged by the military profession—passed into the grand design of his mature thought and took shape in *The War Memoirs* written during the period of his "withdrawal to the desert," 1952-1958. Actually, it is neither history nor recollections of war, but the monumental self-portrait of the solitary man who made himself the champion and knight-servant of "Our Lady France." Each sentence must be taken word for word—even (and indeed especially) in the rhetorical passages and the patriotic clichés—beginning with the celebrated passage at the opening of the *Memoirs*: "All my life I have thought of France in a certain way . . . like the princess of fairy stories . . . dedicated to an exalted and exceptional destiny. . . . Providence has created her for complete successes or for exemplary misfortunes. . . . France is not really herself except in the first rank. . . . In short, to my mind, France cannot be France without *la grandeur*"; and, from early childhood, "I did not doubt that France would have to go through gigantic trials, that life's interest would consist in one day rendering her some signal service, and that I would have that opportunity."

All this still adds up to nothing more than the makings of a first-rate officer of the old French school. What has been joined to the faith which was instilled in the cradle, and what has differentiated de Gaulle from the intellectual environment in which he grew up, is something that at first appears very banal, but which has been decisive: namely, that very early he added to the glories of ancient France the glories of the revolutionary and Napoleonic armies. A monarchist by instinct and molding, he ceased to be one by ideology; indeed, with one stroke he disencumbered himself of all ideology, in order "to serve only France." . . .

For de Gaulle, the philosophy of history and political philosophy are one. The generals of the Revolution and of the Empire "served France well," just as later the Communists in the Resistance and Maurice Thorez (as long as he was a minister under de Gaulle) "served France well." "Is it simply political tactics? The answer is not for me to unravel. For me it is enough that France is served." This ideological indifference, which springs not from opportunism but from unqualified nationalism, is what separated de Gaulle most sharply from all "party men" and what distinguished him as well from most of the leaders of the French army. It made it possible for him to decide in 1940 to break all traditions of discipline, to revolt against the authority and legitimacy of Marshal Pétain, and to proclaim that legitimacy now rested with him, the solitary soldier who picked up "from the mud" and raised anew the flag which had fallen from the hands of his superiors.

He was not anti-Fascist; little did it matter to him who ruled Germany: he refused to admit the defeat of France, and personally, in 1940-1945, he was much less at war with Germany than with the Anglo-Saxon allies who considered that "France was gone." Nor was he anti-Communist when, in 1947, convinced of the imminence of war between Russia and the West, he founded a party whose only ideology was to rally France around himself. He then excluded from the national community all those who put faith in Soviet Russia above patriotism, and in order to point out that this was not a question of ideology, he labeled them, not Communists, but "separatists," or "those

who do not play the game of France." In the same way today
he never speaks of the Soviet Union, but only of Russia, signify-
ing that in his eyes what matters is the eternal Russia, so many
times the ally of France and perhaps an ally again some day;
and that ideologies are only a veil covering the timeless politics
of national power.

Read in the last volume of *The War Memoirs* his portrayal
of Stalin: ". . . astute and implacable champion of a Russia
exhausted by suffering and tyranny but afire with national ambition . . . mightier and more durable than any theory, any regime
. . . to unite the Slavs, to overcome the Germans, to expand in
Asia, to gain access to open seas; these were the dreams of Mother
Russia, these were the despot's goals." But also read the fasci-
nated passage in which de Gaulle wrote of the suicide of Hitler
("So as not to be bound, Prometheus cast himself into the
abyss"): "the terrible greatness of his combat and his memory,"
the "superhuman and inhuman attempt" of that "Titan who
tries to lift the world," and whom Germany had "served with
greater exertions than any people has ever offered any leader."
Each was the embodiment of his nation and played the game of
national ambition, as it is the role of great statesmen to do.

What is true for Hitler or Stalin is also true for Churchill or
Roosevelt. In the same *Memoirs* de Gaulle examines Roosevelt's
conception of how the postwar world should be organized, with
its Directory of the Big Four, i.e. Roosevelt, Stalin, Churchill and
Chiang Kai-shek, of whom the last two, he remarked, were dependent "clients" of the United States. De Gaulle's analysis is
one of the most perspicacious that has been made—not only
because he had reason to resent the American effort to discount
France as a great power, but even more because of his haughty
disdain of the ideological and idealistic aspects of Roosevelt's
grand design. "As is human," de Gaulle wrote, "idealism here
dresses up the will to power." International politics is and will
remain what it has been since there have been rival states in the
world—a game of power politics; and all the rest, ideologies and
contrivances of international organizations, is nothing but mas-

querade and illusion. In this game, it is imperative that France play her cards well and sustain her role.

This view of international politics which, for all its apparent simplicity, is capable of every Machiavellian refinement, has at bottom always been the view taken by the man in the street following in his newspaper the endless conflicts of the "powers," whose leaders clash as often over precedence and prestige as over concrete conflicts of interest. The Gaullist version of this concept springs from European history, or rather from the dramatized, nationalistic version of it which, in the service of patriotic education, the history books of every European nation have imparted to generations of studious youths. It is a complicated history of an equilibrium which was forever in question among powers and coalitions of powers divided one against the other on a narrow continent, where each nation always had to guard its bridges against the enemy of the moment—and against the ally of the moment, who could be the adversary of tomorrow—and where, according to the historiographers who poisoned the minds of generations of Europeans, the increased status of one nation was always paid for by the decline of others.

The United States, which has dominated a vast continent almost from its birth, never knew the problem of "balance of power" until very recently, and then on a global scale. It is this very different historical experience which has resulted in so many misunderstandings between America and Europe, from Versailles to Yalta. But was Roosevelt's reasoning very different when he sought to found the postwar world on the basis of a personal entente among the Big Four of that time? That is the irrational way in which children imagine the world is ruled, and in this respect great statesmen and children are very much alike; nor is their view further from reality than the complicated models of political scientists. Even in the science of international law, until quite recently, Europe could not conceive of international relations except in allegorical terms—as relations between legitimate heads of state. When Europeans of General de Gaulle's generation were growing up, international relations were, in fact and in law, relations between dynastic sovereigns, equal in rank if not in power; and Frenchmen with family traditions such as those of de Gaulle suffered to see Republican France and France alone in Europe, deprived of dynasty—that is, of personification, continuity and dignity.

The postulate of a single strong authority as head of state does not, for de Gaulle, spring from considerations of domestic social order or ideologies; it is an imperative imposed by the realities of international life, which demand that a country be "represented." He was enough of a modernist and a realist to resign himself to the fact that France was no longer a hereditary monarchy, but in his innermost self he never doubted that France needed a monarch—that is to say, an uncontested *chef*—in order to make her voice heard; and the course of events (and his will) finally permitted him to present a monarch to France: himself. His truly monarchical sense of the dignity of the head of state is what strikes one most in his ceremony, in his oratorical style and in his attention to precedence; but this is often misinterpreted. It requires perhaps a feeling for royal tradition to understand how a man can, in all humility, so venerate himself as the incarnation and symbol of his country, as a historical phenomenon distinct from his individual person and of different clay from ordinary men, and subordinate himself so entirely to the "heavy burden" of this self-imposed role which prevents him from ever descending to the level of simple humans; so must the ideal king sacrifice his ego to his royal function. Indeed, de Gaulle has pushed the distinction between himself, "the poor mortal," and Charles de Gaulle, who is invested by history with national legitimacy, to the point of grammatically separating "me" and "de Gaulle," whom he invokes in the third person. In the plebeian world of today, this aspect of his personality is doubtless as uncommon as the appearance of a dinosaur among post-diluvian fauna; and one of the worst mistakes is to confuse him with the vulgar demagogues and rabble-rousers who abound throughout the present-day world. He plays this royal role to perfection and he knows the power of its attraction. There are few Frenchmen, even among those who are irritated by him or who make fun of him, who are not secretly under his spell and who do not experience at least an esthetic satisfaction in seeing France so regally represented after having seen it led so long by men of little stature.

III

What, then, are de Gaulle's policies? They have only one common and consistent thread: to "maintain his status," his and France's, the two being synonymous, "as long as God lends him life." In the key chapter of his *Memoirs*, . . . the words which endlessly recur are "rank," "prestige," "honor," "dignity," "power" and "greatness." As a retrospective exposition of his "great national aims," this apologia of de Gaulle's postwar policy is rather disappointing, and its concrete objectives are now only bad memories: the dismemberment of Germany, the extension of the French frontier to the Rhine, the annexation of the Saar and of some Italian territory, and the stubborn maintenance of the French imperial position in Asia and Africa. The alliance with Stalin, as a stratagem against "the Anglo-Saxon hegemony," remained utterly sterile, and the lofty vision—now revived—of an "association of Slavs, Germans, Gauls and Latins," uniting Europe "from the Atlantic to the Urals," has never meant anything definable. We know only that the aim is to transform the continent into "one of the three planetary powers" which "one day, if necessary, could arbitrate between the Soviet and the Anglo-Saxon camps." Where, then, are the Urals? The common denominator of so many vague or contradictory projects was the high-minded determination to see France "act boldly, achieve stature, and nobly serve the interests of herself and of mankind."

To uphold status is an aristocratic ideal which can fill the life of a man and of a nation. What that ideal requires has less to do with actions than with attitudes. The criteria are simple and easy to understand. "France is only France when she is in the first rank;" she can never accept less; never recognize a hegemony other than her own; never join a group as less than equal with the greatest; never integrate—or rather, "dissolve herself"—in a supranational organization where her veto power would no longer come into play. The Atlantic Alliance may be a good thing, but an "integrated" Atlantic organization under command other than de Gaulle's is unacceptable. A European confederation under French leadership may be desirable, but a United States of Europe in which France might have to give in to the will of the majority is inconceivable. Partnership with the United States is something to be wished for, but an *Atlantic* partnership, in which the United States' partner would not be France, but an integrated Europe, can only be rejected. A United Nations in which France has an assured veto power and a seat in the supreme directory can be useful, but an international organization in which a majority can overrule her is an abomination. Instinctively de Gaulle resists all the bright organizers, all the "technocratic robots" who threaten to depersonalize international relations, just as he instinctively tends to return to the pre-1914 rules of the game, to classical diplomacy, classical alliances, national armaments and the gold standard. Political scientists may debate whether or not these notions are anachronisms in the modern world. But to try to make de Gaulle give in on any of them is to knock one's head against a wall. Those who have to deal with him had better discard in advance any such thoughts as far as France is concerned.

It is true, then, that Gaullist policy—or political style—is more easily defined by what it rejects in contemporary Western politics than by its concrete objectives or constructive proposals. To say no is one of the rare things that one can do all alone. Then, too, history is unforeseeable—"the future lasts a long time and anything can happen one day"—and the wise statesman keeps his hands free to deal with any eventuality; he does not commit himself to anything irrevocable. As long as the symbolic attributes of great-power status are preserved, no material catastrophe can engulf a country. It is the symbols that matter, not the facts: this is the summary of de Gaulle's wartime experience and the essence of his policy. Immediate goals, as well as the means to attain them, can be endlessly adjusted to "the changing nature of things."

When France was faced with the Algiers *putsch* in May 1958, and only de Gaulle's return seemed able to avert a civil war, did he know what he was going to do with the almost unlimited powers he had obtained as a condition for his return? In France, in Algeria and in the French possessions overseas, he called for a vote on a new constitution making him president of the "French Community," and he excommunicated the one territory which did not give him a majority, Guinea. He certainly did not envisage the demise of the Community within two years, without its institutions ever having functioned. Nor did he foresee the loss of Algeria after four years of tortuous maneuvers, riots, pronunciamentos and, finally, the exodus of the French population under the worst possible conditions. But he knew how to submit gallantly to what he could not prevent, and so to enhance France's prestige in the eyes of the Third World. Nor did he imagine that he would fall heir to the European policies of Jean Monnet, Robert Schuman and Guy Mollet, on which he had always showered sarcasm; but he knew how to forge those policies into an instrument of *French* policy, reducing the Common Market to a technical organization from which his ministers were able to draw every advantage for the French economy, while chopping down the political hopes of its creators.

De Gaulle knew how to play every card and keep the public guessing. But in no domain, either domestic or European, has he created anything which is assured of surviving him. The constitution he has given France, with its "president-arbiter" and its "separation of powers," has never functioned and he has not hesitated to recast it or to disregard it when it got in his way, with the result that no one can say how France will be governed after he goes.

If "decolonizer" de Gaulle retains a sort of moral presence in what was the French Community, it is because after the unhappy Guinea experience he consented to finance it on generous terms without ever testing its loyalty—just as he has consented to finance socialist Algeria without insisting on the Évian agreements. But again, no one can say what Franco-Algerian and Franco-African relations will be like when de Gaulle has gone and France perhaps tires of the high cost of prestige. As for Europe, having blocked political integration in the name of national sovereignty and the admission of Britain in the name of political integration, and having attempted to impose a Franco-German directorate (which was bound in advance to fail), he has left the political construction of Europe in an impasse from which it will not emerge so long as he rules, if ever.

The same is true of the Atlantic Alliance. It has been at loggerheads since September 1958 when de Gaulle, just returned to power, proposed a three-power directorate for the global strategy of the West. Implied, of course, was a request for allied support for France's still undefined policy in Africa and Algeria. All the vicissitudes since then have done nothing to reduce the stumbling block created by ill humor; but neither has the ill humor been pushed to the point of rupture. The most obvious result, thus far, is that for the sake of status symbols, de Gaulle has reduced France's potentially great influence inside the Alliance to a mere sulky negativism which has simply to be discounted in advance by her partners. Still, in his eyes, the Alliance is necessary "for a long time to come" in order to maintain equilibrium in the world and in Europe and to cover his retreat while he explores the foggy perspectives of a "European Europe" equilibrated between Paris and Moscow.

In this Gaullist policy of simple ideas and complicated games, everything is provisional; and everything is based on his personal reign. . . . The only certainty is that there will be no one to carry on. Whether the presidency will go to a Pompidou or a Defferre, or whether France will return to parliamentary government or whatever, his successors will have to search for another style and other ways. As with Bismarck, who was successful in everything except assuring the continuation of his work, de Gaulle's policies and personalized rule will end with him. France's partners can no more count on de Gaulle lasting forever than they can avoid living with him while he stays.

But is it really more difficult for France's allies to live with de Gaulle than it was to live with the Fourth Republic, from Bidault to Pflimlin [two of the many French premiers from 1946 to 1958], with its feeble central power, enormous world-wide responsibilities and torn conscience? When we make up a tentative balance sheet for the first seven years of the Fifth Republic, at least one item is certain: with all its jolts and dramatic repudiations, the reign of General de Gaulle has succeeded in drawing France back within her natural boundaries, removing the burden of her imperial heritage which had become too heavy to carry, and making her a European nation, without world-wide involvement—political or strategic. It may not be what he wished, nor what was hoped for by those who carried him to power and who are today in prison, in exile or, in the case of those like Michel Debré who were most faithful to his person and myth, in melancholy retirement. The cost to France—and to Algeria—of the misunderstanding which it took four years to dispel may have been appalling, but the liquidation has been radical and has left nothing but a hangover of sterile rancors. It is futile to speculate whether, if the phenomenon of de Gaulle had never existed to confuse all the issues, the parliamentary republic would in the end have done better or worse in amputating its former North African province: this would be to suppose French history other than it has been since 1940, perhaps less colorful, perhaps more normal. However that may be, it is done; and miraculously de Gaulle has succeeded in transforming into a personal triumph what under any other regime would have appeared to be a catastrophe, and what perhaps no other regime could have survived. Never does the grand manner matter so much as in misfortune; the art of the glorious retreat is the most difficult in war or in politics. Thanks to de Gaulle, thanks to his majestic bearing in times of adversity and to the magic of his language, the regime which "sold out the empire" is in French minds the reign that reestablished the ranking position of France and made the world sit up and take notice.

A NEW FRANCE [2]

The French have for centuries seemed to be endowed, or afflicted, with a capacity—unmatched by any other nation in the

[2] From "A New France: Changes in French Society and Culture," by Henri Peyre, Sterling professor of French at Yale University. *Current History.* 50:193-200. Ap. '66. Reprinted by permission.

West—to resist change and to persevere in a more or less traditional stability. They acclaim novelties in fashion, in the arts, in
literary movements; until recently they thought little of having
governments overturned every six months, a new constitution
voted every three years or another educational reform installed
before an earlier one had been tried. Foreign observers have
called them fickle and unstable—knowing full well that there was
more social stability, bordering on complacent stagnation, in
France than elsewhere in the West. The French elections, except
that which brought a clear majority to Charles de Gaulle in 1962,
have never registered a sharp shift of votes such as has been seen
in Germany and regularly in Britain. In the setting of their daily
lives and in their mental habits, the French have been slow in
"espousing their own age" as their present leader put it, urging
them not to enter into the future backward. . . .

The presidential contest of December, 1965 [won by Charles
de Gaulle], showed that nostalgia for the past has not altogether
disappeared in France. The multi-party confusion and the vehe-
ment reluctance to agree to disagree appear to remain dear to
many. A deep-seated fear of losing one's individuality in a consensus and of boredom still seems to dwell in the collective sub-
conscious of the country. Yet profound changes have taken place
between 1950 and the middle 1960's. They are psychological and
social more than economic and political. The substructure of
France and her moods have been altered.

This change should not be attributed to Gaullism, for the
process began before de Gaulle, under the Fourth Republic.
Gaullism was made possible and became popular because it endorsed the changes which had taken place and because it accelerated them. If, in 1965, it lost its grip upon a substantial minority of the people, it was due to some impatience with the
ominous and cryptic style of an arrogant leader, but also to the
fact that, having reached a high plateau of prosperity, the French
wanted to climb still higher and to share more generously among
all the advantages which had accrued from what many call
"Americanization."

Inquiries, questionnaires and statistics, especially in a country which has traditionally distrusted these methods, fail to reveal the extent of the psychological changes which are now transforming French society. Excessive reliance on these methods was in part responsible for the gross mistakes committed by observers of France in 1950-1958, who practically wrote France off as the chronic invalid of Europe. It hid from them—under an umbrella of apparent submersion in volatile politics and the obstinately insoluble problems of Indochina and North Africa—the immense progress actually being achieved.

French society has and is being altered by the habit of prosperity, by a mood of confidence in its future, by a sense (perhaps deceptive) of security, since for the first time in half a century the country is neither at war nor fears the oncoming of a war, as well as by a shift of the population away from tilling the soil to industry, technology and the professions.

Facts and figures have been profusely displayed in American weeklies, in *The Economist* [a prominent British publication] and in Swiss and German papers to illustrate the miraculous progress effected since 1950. British observers have noted, at times with a little spite, that their Gallic neighbors seemed to have struck a way "to spend themselves rich" and that their rate of steady growth has been twice as fast as that of "moral" Britain. . . . The progress, however, was actually largely due, at least at the start, to American assistance in gifts, loans and knowhow. It was due also to a happy conjunction of events that took place over the years.

The nightmare of being deficient in coal, which had obsessed the French for a century, was dispelled when hydroelectric energy and oil became greater assets than coal. Even steel, in which Britain and Germany outproduced France, became relatively less important, as chemicals, electronics, new alloys and plastics became more so. France stands high (fourth) in the world among the producers of uranium. Figures are eloquent and tell part of the story. In ten years, coal will be down from 76 per cent to 28 per cent as a source of the total power used in France. Consumption of oil, much of it from Africa, is being paid more and more in francs and no longer drains dollars away. In 1965, consumption of electric energy was double what it had been in 1955. Forty-three per cent of French families in 1964 had a car, as against 21 per cent in 1954; 34 per cent had TV instead of one per cent in 1954; 47 per cent had a refrigerator as against 7.5 per cent and 35 per cent a washing machine as against 8.4 per cent in 1954.

The daily life and the structure of society in France have naturally been affected by these changes. The share of food in the total expense of French families has gone down from 49 per cent in 1950 to 38.7 per cent in 1963; less also is spent on clothes; but more is expended on housing, machinery and health. The savings in the state saving banks . . . have increased 400 per cent in ten years. The treasury had a comfortable gold reserve of over $5 billion in 1965 and it is still increasing. Taxes, in a country often maligned—by others and itself—as evading them, bring a surplus in the budget. The 1966 budget was voted (with a surplus) as far ahead of time as October 31, 1965.

Social Consequences

But the real significance of this great economic progress lies in the social consequences it has entailed for France. Labor unrest has not been conspicuous in the last decade, except for a miners' strike in 1964 which was not handled skillfully by the government and which in effect voiced the fears of the miners whose role in the total economy is threatened as coal is being replaced by other fuel. It is often not realized that the proportion of industrial workers who belong to the once all-powerful CGT (Confédération Générale du Travail) is now relatively low (1.5 million in 1964 as against 5.5 million in 1946) and is conspicuously small in the new industries: oil, electronics, chemicals. The "alienation" of the workmen from the community is becoming an old-fashioned concept, as the working class—disposing of consumer goods in abundance, buying electrical appliances, automobiles (of which there is a higher percentage per capita than in any other European country), purchasing durable goods on installment—now easily feels the equal of the once superior bourgeois class.

The Communist vote still amounts to slightly over one fifth of the electorate; but the number of party members is only one fourth of what it was after the Liberation, while the party's policies are vacillating and contradictory. It is suspected that a sizable proportion of nominal Communists voted for de Gaulle repeatedly; the prestige of Russia, which was at its highest in 1943-1948, has steadily waned with the fissions in the Communist bloc and the downgrading of Russian agricultural and military power in world opinion since 1962. The presidential elections of December, 1965 [when de Gaulle failed to gain an outright majority and was forced into a run-off election in which he won 55 per cent of the vote—Ed.], have dispelled the myth of de Gaulle's invincibility; but they have also underlined the powerlessness of the French Left to offer anything else than a negative program. The votes which were collected by de Gaulle's opponents (Communists, Socialists, Radicals, Catholics and Rightists) could never have united on a common policy. A labor party, . . . gathering the electors of the working classes, the liberal intellectuals and disregarding the clerical issue, remains an impossibility in France, and apparently elsewhere on the continent. More well-being . . . which has become the new motto, is certainly desired by the working classes; but their wages have increased—especially in the private sector—and the cost of living remained practically steady in 1964-1965 when moves to curb inflation brought about a slight recession. There are fewer than thirty thousand unemployed, less than one per cent of the labor force, and these are from the industries (naval construction, textiles) where the need for modernization is most crying.

The most remarkable social and psychological change, in a nation . . . where griping and declaiming against the government are a time-honored tradition and optimism is taken to be a sign of naïveté, is in the now openly declared confidence about the future. Gaston Berger, an industrialist who has become a professor of philosophy, the eminent political thinker, Bertrand de Jouvenel . . . and many others in France have lately been attempting, not only to forecast the future, but, within limits, to control it. French opinion was impressed in 1965 by a collective work done by the National Commission for the Organization of the Territory: that committee, made up of sober research specialists in economic sociology, concluded that, by 1985, France would have a population of 60 million people, half of them or more under thirty-five years of age; that the Frenchman would then be the richest man in Europe with the national output trebled, the agrarian population down to 2 million, less than 10 per cent of a 22 million labor force.

Another nightmare, even blacker than the dearth of coal, has cast a pall of gloom over the French mind for eighty years: the certainty that, with their population stagnant, they could never face Germany on an equal footing. That fear has now vanished. Germany appears to be divided for many years to come and, with the French birthrate now being considerably higher than the German, and than the European average, France will soon be a younger country, with more people reaching conscription age every year than once-dreaded Germany.

That factor, and the realization that, industrially and commercially, France has more than held her own in the Common Market [composed of France, West Germany, Italy, Belgium, the Netherlands and Luxembourg] relative to Germany account for the prevailing sense of security. The contrast with the anxiety which demoralized France between 1933 and 1939 is sharp indeed. Anguish serves as a fashionable theme in today's literature and dissertations on the absurd still follow in the wake of [writers such as] Camus, Beckett and Ionesco, but few signs of genuinely lived anguish are discernible among French youth.

The new military bill, much to the dismay of the old guard and after being twice turned down by the Senate, was voted in 1965. It provides for many exemptions from the draft [and] a standing army down to less than 50 per cent of its number in 1962 . . . . The old concepts of war which used to be traditional in Europe have been exploded: struggles waged on the battlefield, the taking of prisoners, the disarming of the enemy, and the occupation of his homeland. The present-day desire of the French is not to expand their army, which would merely serve as cannon fodder in the face of foes equipped with advanced aviation and atomic bombs, or which might encourage the Americans to withdraw their own forces from Europe. They do not seriously believe that Russia will constitute a threat to Western Europe for at least a decade or that either of the superpowers will resort to the use of the bomb; but they, like the Germans, are wary of an agreement between America and Russia which would cease to use the threat as a possible means of deterrence.

Other changes which have gradually altered French society in the last decade are: the strengthening of the middle class and, in spite of the loud proclamations of existentialist philosophers, the weakening of the Hegelian "unhappy conscience" with which the bourgeoisie may have been afflicted between the two world wars; the growing freedom of women and the consequent new spirit in which the relations between the two sexes are envisaged; and the profound transformation of the peasantry.

Class and Marriage in France

It is a mistake frequently made in America to imagine, from the reading of Balzac, Flaubert and Mauriac and from an insidious absorption of the Marxist critique of society, that the stratification of the classes in France is very rigid, that intermarriages (cutting across religious, economic, social or racial hurdles) are a rare occurrence, and that the middle class is uniformly sclerosed, complacent and selfish, hence doomed. The fortunes of the upper bourgeoisie have repeatedly been undermined by inflation and by all the loans made by France to foreign countries which never repaid them. Access to all the advantages once enjoyed by the privileged middle class (secondary and higher education, long vacations and travel abroad, epicurean tastes) has long been granted to all. Education is free at all levels and if there are relatively very few sons and grandsons of industrial and agrarian workers studying in the universities, there are many of their grandsons and great grandsons; the usual procedure has been for the sons first to become modest schoolteachers or minor employees and then to raise their children above their own level. The failure of nerve which undermined the bourgeoisie for a time has disappeared. That class, an open, loose and flexible one, is constantly being renovated through infusion of new elements from below. . . . It has produced a very large majority of the vigorous leaders in most professions, the most inventive technicians, the most gifted artists and writers, including those who, like Mauriac, Malraux, Breton, Sartre, and de Gaulle himself (who, since his family was always poor and lived in relative insecurity, has declared that he never felt at one with the bourgeoisie), have often maligned the very group from which they stemmed.

According to several recent inquiries by sociologists, . . . young marriages have become standard procedure in France: the average age is 21 for women, 24 for men. The couples meet at dances, winter sports, summer resorts, and more and more while working together as students, as social workers, or in church activities. The marriages are no longer arranged by the families but they are approved by them in 80 per cent of the cases. Nine weddings out of ten are accompanied by a church ceremony. The proportion of married women having a profession other than housewife is, next to that of Russia, the highest of any country. Of 18.2 million French women over fifteen, 6.6 million, in 1964, had a job other than housewife or in addition to that of housewife. The concept of the wife as *camarade,* of the girl going out with young men and splitting expenses (the practice of steady dating has not yet afflicted the French youth) has spread widely today. The comradeship, however, means sharing on the part of the wife more than by the male, who still resists assisting with household chores and who often is encouraged in this by his wife, who seems to fear that he might lose some of his virility thereby and some of the respect which the children should entertain for him. In 1965, another breach was made on the Code Napoleon when it was voted that the rights of married women would be vastly enlarged: they can now retain the property they owned before marriage, hold a job without the husband's consent and enjoy full financial autonomy. At the same time, the old-fashioned practice of the dowry is gradually disappearing.

The Peasantry

An even more drastic change has taken place in the peasantry. . . . The agricultural population at one time counted approximately 50 per cent of the French people and for years it was customary for the French, and for foreign observers of France, to praise the "classical" solidity and stability afforded by such a harmonious balance between agriculture and industry, the forces of the past and those of modern technology. As late as 1954, rural employment still amounted to 27.3 per cent of the labor force; it was down to 20 per cent in 1963. Cooperatives have been developed, the regrouping of land has been organized, improved efficiency through modernization has doubled, or trebled, production. There were 35,000 tractors in use in 1948, there are 800,000 or more today; there were 260 combines (harvester-thresher), today there are over 60,000; the use of fertilizers is up 300 per cent.

The results are clear: first, France has joined the ranks of the countries (America, Canada, Argentina, Australia) for which the exporting of a substantial part of their agrarian production (grains, cheese, fruits, vegetables, even butter and, some years, meat) is a question of life or death. No government can afford to sacrifice the outlets for its peasantry; several riots of peasants in Brittany, in Provence, in Languedoc, in 1961 and 1963, brought this fact home. Of all the countries of Western Europe, France has an unrivaled capacity for the expansion of her farm production and she cannot jeopardize that position when negotiating with her Common Market partners or with Britain. Her peasants have thus had to forsake their reactionary turn of mind and their attachment to old routines, whereas they had never shown much political maturity before and had voted placidly for old-fashioned radicalism. Suddenly they have realized their power; they produce leaders and lobbyists and join unions. Social security has been extended to six million agricultural workers. The "Complementary Law to the Law of Agricultural Orientation," passed on July 27, 1962, has provided for the recovery by the state, for the profit of the farmers, of untilled land and even of abandoned or unkept houses in the villages, . . . for the reparceling of small areas cut up through the Napoleonic Code and for the prevention of the buying up of too much land . . . by wealthy landowners. The psychological attitudes of the peasantry as well as their relative place in French society have changed more since 1948 or 1950 than they had for a hundred years before.

All these changes have virtually turned an old and traditionalist country into a new France. The French are not always aware of it; they insist on stressing all that remains to be done and on blaming their government for failing to accomplish it fast enough. Yet the chances are that future historians will view de Gaulle's France as having done more toward an actually lived socialism than any earlier regime or Popular Front. More has been achieved by Edgar Pisani, de Gaulle's energetic minister of agriculture, than by any of his predecessors of the Third and Fourth Republics, as the London *Economist* acknowledged in an article of July 27, 1963, on "The Vanishing Peasant." The London *Times Literary Supplement,* in 1964, blandly chided the glib allusions to France as the "sick man" of Europe and added: "The virtual failure of British postwar economic policy has occurred during a decade when the French have achieved an economic growth no less miraculous than that of the Western Germans." The American *Bulletin of Atomic Scientists* of October, 1964, stressing the thorough transformation of French society, remarked: "France, formerly a conservative society of small shopkeepers and industrialists with the lowest rate of economic growth and of population increase in Europe, has been converted into a rapidly growing nation with ambitious economic planning on a national scale, a growing base of high-grade scientific research and a growing readiness to use new technologies. . . ." Further, de Gaulle's premier, Georges Pompidou, declared on September 16, 1964, before the French National Assembly: "France has a socialist economy and it is here to stay."

Education Today

Education has never ceased to be under discussion in France. Parents take a lively personal interest in the schools, the syllabi

of studies, the quality of the teachers, the sacrosanct baccalaureat.
. . . Teachers are divided into several categories (primary, technical, secondary, university), each highly jealous of its prerogatives, clamoring for reforms provided they affect other sectors than their own. Much grumbling is heard against the government's latest attempts at reorganization which have lacked consistency and clarity. But the criticism is negative. No alternative to the reforms now being achieved has been constructively formulated.

The Fourth Republic, in its thirteen years evolved theoretical projects which were never seriously debated, for fear of antagonizing one or another of the parties which made up its frail and shifting majority. Today's Fifth Republic has not done enough, but the whole substructure of the country is nevertheless being altered through some of its educational reforms, accomplished under the pressure of events. The main changes may be summed up thus:

1. Huge increases in the educational budget of the country: from 2 billion francs in 1952 and 4 billion in 1957, the budget jumped to 17 billion for 1966 (easily equivalent to 10 or 11 billion of the 1957 value). Scientific research, which received 179 million in 1958, will receive 1,298 million in 1966, an increase of 620 per cent. The strongest reason behind the adoption of the nuclear and space programs, initiated by the Fourth Republic and pursued by de Gaulle, lies neither in the pursuit of prestige nor of military efficiency (although it was necessary to pacify a disgruntled army after independence was granted to Algeria): it lies in the wish to give a strong impetus to French science through research contracts arranged, as in the United States, by the army.

2. Adoption in 1964, after years of debate, of the old projects for the École Unique, providing for a more democratic primary teaching and for the easier access of a much larger number of children of modest means to secondary and higher education. Secondary teaching, which counted 70,000 children in 1900, will have 3 million in 1970. It is free. Next to Sweden, France is the European country in which the highest number of children continue from primary to secondary education. France turns out three

times more *bacheliers* [secondary school graduates] than Western Germany. Twice as many students as in Britain enter the universities after secondary studies, although this is not an unmitigated good, for the less competent of those, especially in the sciences, eventually fail and are a drag on the others and a burden to the professors. Similarly, the number of girls who go on to the faculties of letters is twice as high as that of the males; hence there are too many students in these faculties (137,000 in 1964-1965), and only 129,000 (when more would be desirable, and two thirds are men) in the faculties of sciences.

3. Much building of schools has been done in the last four years; the increase in professors and assistants at the higher (or university) level has been greater proportionately than that of students. Still Paris—the Sorbonne, with its new faculties lately opened at Nanterre, the Halle aux Vins, the Halle aux Cuirs—is overcrowded. Out of 300,000 university students in France (over one fourth of them on scholarship), 100,000 are in Paris. The astronomical figure of 750,000 is forecast for 1970. Luckily, since 1962, the rate of increase has been higher at the universities of Strasbourg (68 per cent), Aix (50 per cent), Lyon (50 per cent), Dijon (40 per cent) than at Paris.

4. The baccalaureate has undergone changes, not always for the better, far too often since 1958. The general trend however is toward more sciences, less stress on Latin, more room given to economic and social studies. Far more remains to be achieved. Economics remains wedded, at the university level, to the law schools and is too theoretical. Too much teaching in France is overly rigid and overly abstract. The ruling classes, between 1929 and 1939, committed grievous mistakes because they knew far too little about inflation, deflation, devaluation, Keynesian economics, the need for mass production.

5. The excessive rigidity of French educational and social structures is now being broken down through a number of ways in which the baccalaureate may be bypassed. Engineers at a high level are very highly and scientifically trained in France and are in fact more numerous than in West Germany. But the crying need is for many more superior technicians, trained in

two years, as opposed to the more mathematically trained engineers whose training lasts from three to seven years. Ten Instituts Universitaires de Technologie are to be opened in 1966: some already exist—at Lyon, Toulouse, Rennes and Lille, as a beginning.

6. An original feature of French education, and one of the factors which have characterized the whole of the French society over generations, is the Grandes Écoles: École Normal Supérieure (80 admitted yearly), École Polytechnique (300), École Nationale d'Administration (80). The elite of France, which constitutes the backbone of the country, is trained there. This open elite is far more educational and cultural than hereditary or social. . . . British observers of France have lately expressed their admiration for the French training of an elite of civil servants. One of these British observers has credited the remarkable social and economic achievement of France, in spite of parliamentary instability, and de Gaulle's subsequent achievement, to that "cadre of high functionaries, . . . often astonishingly young, . . . in whom class consciousness has been replaced by a sort of caste consciousness based on their educational success and their privileges of power."

The Arts

Another article would be needed to include a sketch of literature and the arts in France over the last decade. French achievement in the arts is the one best known in the United States where new French books are voraciously read and translated, French music is played generously, French art is shown and bought though often criticized by American art critics anxious to serve the prestige of their own New York and California schools. Strangely enough, while the country is going through a tremendous social and psychological upheaval, . . . displaying faith in itself and in the future, and not a little arrogance in its attitude to the rest of the world, literature seems to indulge pessimism, portrays impotence, morbidity, Hamlet-like doubts about itself and masochistically reviles the very concept of literature. An ironical paradox is that, while the president is by far the greatest master of literary prose to have occupied the symbolic throne of France for centuries and prizes intellectuals (Malraux, Joxe, Debré, Jean-neney, et al., all authors) above the militaries whom, except for Mauriac, he scorns, the outstanding French writers of today who may some day be called the luminaries of the Gaullist age are all adverse to him: Sartre, Aragon, Robbe-Grillet, Butor, Simone de Beauvoir, Violette Leduc, or indifferent to his appeals for grandeur and glory.

The achievement of the Division of Cultural Relations at the Ministry of Foreign Affairs have been significant: over 30,000 French teachers serve abroad in Africa, North America and else-where. There are 66 cultural counselor posts abroad, 8 of them including a scientific attaché; 177 French *lycées* and colleges abroad, attended by over 300,000 pupils at the secondary level. Over 40,000 foreign students study in France. Book exports in-creased 10 per cent in 1964 over the preceding year and represent 20 per cent of French book production. The French effort in this domain is more energetic, and more generously provided, than that of any other country. It was endorsed on June 10, 1964, by the adoption of the second plan for cultural expansion abroad.

In France, where André Malraux is in charge of what is called "Cultural Affairs," . . . national theaters have been reorganized and their subsidy has been raised from 23 million francs in 1959 to nearly 54 million in 1966. Buildings have been cleaned and renovated. The prestige of artists has been enhanced by national funerals in great state arranged for Braque and Le Corbusier, and by official orders for the decorating of ceilings to Chagall and André Masson. TV has brought about a severe crisis for the cinema, which is not yet over. But the chief char-acter of cultural life has been in its decentralization. Paris is no longer the cradle of innovations. Much admired Maisons de la Culture have been opened at Havre, Caen, Ménilmontant and at Bourges. Over twelve dramatic centers are active in the prov-inces and music festivals are mushrooming in as many cities. For the first time in a century and a half, the attraction of Paris as the magnet for intellectuals and artists and as a crucible for all innovations has paled and many professors and innovators choose to stay in the provinces and to teach or experiment there.

Progress in Latin countries, and indeed in the greater part of a world in which the Anglo-Saxons and the Scandinavians remain a minority, has often been achieved through revolutions rather than through a gradual evolution. A great many minor changes are thus crystallized into a more momentous upheaval, individual wills are magnetized and, once drastic moves forward have occurred, a period of assimilation of these changes follows. It may well be that the French, after a prolonged seven-year itch of stability, are, in 1966, feeling nostalgic for some turbulence. The tone of a leader who is convinced of his own infallibility and his imperious style of action may well pall on them. They have achieved security, economic advance, social peace, freedom from fear of war in Europe and of colonial wars, scientific progress and a truly democratic education for all. . . .

But the profound modifications which have been effected in the social structure and in the mental adaptation of the French people to the modern world are likely to stay, as will probably a fair degree of governmental stability and of executive predominance over a rule by an assembly. France has gone a longer way to adapt herself to the technological world of today within the twenty years since she emerged, scarred and impoverished, from German occupation than she had traveled for a full century.

DE GAULLE BRINGS STABILITY [3]

Contrasted with the bevy of competing political figures in the Fourth Republic [which preceded the present Fifth Republic], the emergence of one man who is acknowledged by followers and antagonists alike as the national leader is certainly a new and striking factor for political stability. In addition, provisions for greater stability have been incorporated into the political institutions of the Fifth Republic. The office of the presidency, hand-tailored for de Gaulle, has been endowed with new strength and prestige. The president is not selected by direct election, but

[3] From *France Under de Gaulle*, pamphlet by the late E. S. Furniss, Jr., professor of politics and author. (Headline Series no 139) Foreign Policy Association. 345 E. 46th St. New York 10017. Ja. '60. p 12-18. Copyright 1960 by Foreign Policy Association, Inc. Reprinted by permission.

rather chosen by some 81,000 French and overseas legislators and local French officials. Thus both the conservative nature and the indirect public responsibility of the president are ensured.

The office of the presidency carries with it direct and indirect powers. Without the accompanying signature of the premier, the president may dissolve Parliament and submit proposals to popular referendum after consultation with the premier and the president of the assemblies. He is the presiding head of the French Community. Most controversial of all his powers is his right under Article 16 of the constitution to assume control, after official consultation with the premier, the presidents of the assemblies and the constitutional committee, in the event he believes "the institutions of the Republic, the independence of the nation, the integrity of its territory or the fulfillment of its international commitments are threatened in a grave and immediate manner" and when the regular functioning of the constitutional governmental authorities is interrupted. The president's indirect authority derives from the fact that it is he who selects in fact as well as in theory "his" premier (in the past the premier was chosen by the National Assembly) and has a hand in the appointment of other members of the government. Combined with the president's independent prerogatives, this means that a strong personality, such as de Gaulle, can virtually assure that the "government," meaning the premier and his cabinet, is the executor of the policies he devises.

President Central Figure

An additional contribution to increased stability is the changed relationship between executive and legislative branches. The National Assembly of the French Republic was deliberately created to control the executive. The result was a political system both impotent and irresponsible: impotent because the Assembly, unable itself to govern, would not permit the executive to do so; irresponsible because the lines of authority were so discontinuous and diffuse that it was impossible to assess, let alone to exact, accountability for national action or inaction.

In place of this weak construction, whose only merit was that it faithfully reflected the divisions and antagonisms prevailing among French political groups, de Gaulle and his followers, notably Debré, had long advocated a separation of powers and a reversal of relative authority assigned to the executive and the legislature. What has emerged in the Fifth Republic, however, is only a partial separation of powers. While the president owes nothing in his position to the legislature, and the members of the government must resign their seats when they assume ministerial office, the premier, along with his cabinet, may be overturned by the National Assembly in two circumstances. He can voluntarily stake his government's life on a particular measure—a pale reflection of the former vote of confidence—or the Assembly can pass a motion of censure. The introduction of such a motion requires the signature of one tenth of the Assembly's membership. Passage requires an absolute majority. This ends the practice of passive disapproval, for those who abstain are, in effect, voting for the government. Although nothing in the constitution so dictates, Premier Debré may have established a precedent when [in 1959], upon designation by de Gaulle, he asked the Assembly to approve himself and his ministers. Later in the Assembly session the government revealed a use to which confidence votes may be put. Under the Fourth Republic, particularly at budget time, the cabinets not infrequently threatened to resign, leaving France with only a caretaker executive. By contrast, the decision to ask for a vote on de Gaulle's Algerian policy—which was endorsed 441-23 on October 26, 1959—was clearly devised to force restive deputies back into line, with the cabinet remaining in control.

Whips and Prods

To ensure that the Assembly no longer treats premiers and ministers with the casual irreverence that was customary under the Fourth Republic, the government has been handed several whips for the recalcitrant and prods for the reluctant. Premiers of the Fifth Republic will control the debates and actions of the Assembly from the moment the sitting begins to the day of adjournment. If, as is very unlikely, a special session is voted, it must disband after exhausting a specified agenda or after twelve days. Deputies collaborating in an unsuccessful motion of censure may not do so again, and all deputies must vote. Thus destruction of government by absence or by proxy is not permitted.

The first Assembly, even though largely composed of professed antiparliamentarians, thought it had detected a chink in the executive's armor—the right to interpellation. If, after questioning the executive, a debate and vote should ensue, the Assembly would have a means to voice its disapproval without suffering the consequences of a ministerial crisis or, possibly, dissolution. More important, it might so expand this chink that the executive would ultimately become self-consciously responsive to legislative threats. Debré's government, recognizing the possible inroads on executive authority, made an issue of the Assembly rules and ultimately succeeded in limiting interpellation to a questioning, not a test, of the executive.

Use of Executive Decrees

The first regular session of the National Assembly ended on July 27, 1959 with the lower house having done what the executive wanted and no more. If conflicts should occur in the future between the legislature and the executive, the Fifth Republic provides a safeguard familiar to France, that is, legislative grants to the executive of the right to issue decrees, which can be nullified only by explicit action by the Assembly. Should the Assembly and the Senate join forces to oppose the government, the executive may intervene to put an end to the shuttling of bills between them. In the case of finance bills both houses must act within seventy days or the executive may issue ordinances incorporating the various measures. This means that if the rulers of the Fifth Republic are determined, they can surprise France and the Western world by establishing the annual budget before the advent of each fiscal year. No government of the preceding regime was able to do this, and the sad spectacle of a major nation living from hand to mouth for months at a time was an important factor in the decline of the repute of French governments at home and abroad.

After de Gaulle, What?

Institutional as well as personal factors, then, are at work to make the Fifth Republic a stable system new for France. There are, however, several counteracting tendencies which emerge in the process of analyzing this new system. One obvious question concerns de Gaulle himself. How long can he continue to chart, not just the general direction for France, but the detailed course which the nation in all its affairs, both foreign and domestic, is to follow? If the office is a formidable one, designed for a formidable man, it will by that very token be a large vacuum to fill if and when the aging president's vigor and vision begin to falter.

Moreover, de Gaulle is but one segment of this strong executive, which consists of two distinct components—president and premier. Other prospects for tension arise from the role to be played in the Fifth Republic by the premier and his ministers. It is not likely that the attempt by the Assembly to dominate the government will cease. . . . The very fact that the executive is so powerful will also inspire individuals and groups outside the political process to make sure that national policy reflects their interests and that the legislature resumes its traditional position as a source of leverage.

Nor can one expect a premier to remain simply the tractable handmaiden of the president, particularly if the president himself should weaken. To see that the government does in fact, as Article 20 states, "determine and direct the policy of the nation," the premier may well seek sources of power independent of the president wherever he can find them. Two obvious possibilities are first, the legislature, particularly the Assembly, and second, the country at large.

In the first instance a premier may find it in his own interest to team up with an Assembly if its objective is the same as his, even though the president is opposed. Groups within the Assembly can be carefully cultivated so that it is in reality the premier who directs the execution of policy, while at the same time he participates in its formulation. The constitutional provisions of the Fifth Republic encourage such a development, since the premier is far closer to the movements of politics than the aloof, indirectly elected president. In communion with himself the president is to define the national will and serve as its exponent. But national will in the sense of a unified, common desire hardly exists on matters apart from the urge for survival. It is the function of politics to blend and balance partly harmonious, partly divergent, desires which can only to a limited extent be clearly expressed, and forge out of them national action which factions possessing the most power will accept. In this sense the premier must be a politician, as the president cannot be.

What Will Public Support?

So long as de Gaulle retains his tight control over the executive and his great personal popularity throughout the country, it is not likely that his prerogatives will be usurped. Over the long run, however, it would be wise not to forget that the rational turn of mind which drives Frenchmen to search for the perfect constitution is part of the same quality which leads them to regard all the institutions produced by that search as only temporarily deserving of their support.

THE ONCE AND FUTURE KING [4]

Back in 1924 when Charles de Gaulle was a lowly captain of infantry, his colonel, in an otherwise complimentary fitness report, accused the young officer of displaying "the attitude of a king in exile." The only change that the intervening years seem to have made is that de Gaulle no longer feels himself in exile.

It has become *de rigueur* amongst cartoonists all over the world to portray de Gaulle as a twentieth-century reincarnation of Louis XIV, the "Sun King." And de Gaulle (who has even

[4] From article "By Word and Deed, the Once and Future King." *Newsweek*. 66:43. D. 13, '65. Copyright, Newsweek, Inc., December, 1965. Reprinted by permission.

been called the "Sun President") constantly nourishes the caricature by both word and deed. Coldly impervious toward all other mortals, the general follows his own dictum (laid down years ago in *The Edge of The Sword*) that "the leader must . . . be swathed in robes of nobility" in order to "establish his authority over the generality of men who splash in shallow water." At de Gaulle's instigation, the Élysée state functions have been transformed into glittering rituals out of an earlier century. And his periodic trips into the provinces have been dubbed "Good King Charles among his people."

Speedy Service: Inevitably, all this has given rise to considerable irreverent merriment amongst those who regard the general as less than a demigod. In a recent book called *The King and His Court,* French journalist Pierre Viansson-Ponté detailed some of the minor consequences of de Gaulle's regal approach to existence. Because the general is a remarkably rapid eater, the waiters at formal Élysée dinners serve and remove courses with such speed that some guests never even get a bite of their entree. The menu at such affairs, moreover, never includes cheese or fruit—because the general finds cheese malodorous and fruit too time-consuming to peel.

The pageantry and highly personal flavor of the Gaullist regime, of course, are there for all to see. What is not so obvious —because it is hidden away with the Élysée—is a far more substantial consequence of de Gaulle's penchant for the monarchical style. This is the general's "invisible government" composed of some forty devoted and highly gifted men who fulfill a role quite unlike that of presidential advisers in any other Western democracy. Ostensibly, the function of this staff is to provide the general with information, advice, plans and options which will allow him to make policy decisions. But much as did some seventeenth-century kings, de Gaulle uses his personal aides to undercut his official cabinet ministers and thus augment his own power.

Shadows: Having, through his custom-tailored constitution, reduced the French National Assembly to little more than a vestigial organ, and having gradually sliced away the policy-making powers of his cabinet, de Gaulle has carried the process a step further by creating what is, in effect, a parallel government responsible only to him. Each of some fifteen Élysée "shadows" (they are all but unknown to the public) is responsible for one or more of the policy areas that roughly correspond to ministries. Often, de Gaulle calls upon his aides to produce memoranda on current subjects which he can then use to talk down a minister. Or it may be that a minister will submit a memorandum urging action which the general does not want to take. In that case, de Gaulle merely calls for a parallel—and presumably contradictory—memo from the appropriate "shadow." (Such memos must be produced not only with dazzling speed but also in dazzling literary style. The written word, in fact, is the chief tool of the technocrats since de Gaulle loathes the telephone and finds it easier to absorb information visually than in conversation.)

By any standards, the "shadows" of the "invisible government" are an extraordinary group. Tough-minded, suave, lean and hard, they are exceptionally well-educated; most are products of France's elite *grandes écoles* and have previously served in the top-notch French civil service. They are youthful . . . and their loyalty to the general is absolute.

Among the top members of the "invisible government" are: Georges Galichon, fifty, who handles de Gaulle's personal affairs and appointments; Vice Admiral Jean Philippon, fifty-six, who oversees de Gaulle's nuclear *force de frappe* and other defense matters; and Jacques Foccart, fifty-two, a balding ex-parachutist and old Gaullist faithful who nominally heads the department of African and Malagasy affairs but whose real job is the management of the Gaullist secret service. (Foccart is said to have at least six hundred agents under his command—some of them drawn from the French underworld—and has masterminded such coups as the 1963 kidnaping in Munich of ex-Colonel Antoine Argoud, a fanatic anti-Gaullist implicated in a plot against the general.)

Nerve Center: At the very top of the "invisible government," however, stands Étienne Burin des Roziers, fifty-two, who, in view of his closeness to de Gaulle and his intimate knowledge of all that goes on in the government, is probably the second most influential man in France. Oxford-educated and a Gaullist since June 1940, Burin is the Élysée's nerve center; he reads all diplomatic cables, all drafts of new laws and all memoranda prepared for the general. He attends all cabinet and sub-cabinet meetings. His office is one of the few in the Élysée to open directly onto the general's. And, just as important, he regulates the work of the "shadows" in their ceaseless sparring with the official government of France.

To opponents of the Gaullist regime, the "invisible government" in the Élysée seems the perfect device for an autocratically minded leader who wishes to rule both secretly and absolutely. And even some less hostile Frenchmen condemn it as essentially antidemocratic. "Insofar as there is any real and consistent governmental machinery—other than de Gaulle himself—for formulating policy in the Fifth Republic," says one eminent French journalist, "it lies in the Élysée's invisible men."

AT HOME, DE GAULLE STANDS TALL [5]

If President Johnson had President de Gaulle's opinion polls to carry around in his pocket, he would be a happy man. Two out of three Frenchmen—precisely, 65 per cent—are "satisfied" with President de Gaulle, according to the latest survey of the French Institute of Public Opinion. This is a good 10 per cent more than actually voted for him last December, and would be comforting to any president with mid-term parliamentary elections coming up.

The elections here will probably not come before March [1967]. It is up to the president to set the date. But already the campaign is underway, and already some die-hard opponents are deploring that the man looks unbeatable.

To the American eye it might be puzzling that a man can be simultaneously so irritating, or worse, and so popular. It could be pointed out that this same man appears quite reasonable to

[5] From article by Richard E. Mooney, staff reporter. New York *Times.* p E 3. O. 9, '66. © 1966 by The New York Times Company. Reprinted by permission.

some other countries. The essential point, of course, is that what the outside world thinks of a man need bear no relation to what his own country thinks of him.

The fact is, his country—or a large part of it—thinks well of him. Why? Dwight Eisenhower's "Peace and Prosperity" formula comes to mind first. General de Gaulle got France out of its most recent war, in Algeria, and for the first time in a quarter century, France is at peace. Considering that both world wars devastated French territory and crippled her population, war is an affair of the home for France, not some thing that happens on the far side of the ocean.

Prosperity goes almost without saying. The country's over-all output has doubled, and the individual Frenchman's share of this larger pie has risen by more than one half at the same time. But statistics are dry. France is at last entering the consumer age. Everyman has a job, a car, a four-week vacation, and money to spend.

To a Frenchman it all adds up to stability. Granted that most men's memories do not run back many decades, it is only necessary to look back to the last one. There was France's war in Indochina, and then in Algeria. There were governments changing with the calendar. There was inflation and several devaluations of the franc.

De Gaulle's Role

And then came the general.

To be sure, many serious Frenchmen believe that General de Gaulle is ruining their country, not saving it. The political institutions of France . . . have been enfeebled by the power of the president. The political opposition may be a little less fractionated than it was, but it has lost its traditional vitality. Men argue about whether France has become a dictatorship, and decide that it hasn't—but the question comes up. And, finally, all of France sees, approving or not, that their president is cutting their country off from historic friends—not to mention benefits— in the Western world.

In fact, the general's position in world politics today is one of his strengths. For some people, he has restored pride in French greatness. But, less romantically, for many people it is a simple case of agreeing with the stands he takes. It is commonplace to hear that it is not the general's policies which are offensive, it's his manner.

Above all, the continuing war in Vietnam strengthens him. It is not a popular war in any country, but among the major Western countries it is only in France that the country's president is stirring up the unpopularity.

The war, aside from being an issue itself, supports much of the rest of his fractiousness with the Western alliance, and particularly with the United States, of course. It would be a rash man who campaigned for French office today on an all-out pro-American platform. The European unity issue has been sufficiently fuzzed up to make it a difficult campaign issue, at best, and General de Gaulle's negotiators in the European Common Market have taken care of the large French farm population very generously.

Finally, the Communists. It is not sinful in France to be friendly with Communists. The Communists are the largest single political party here, except for the Gaullist Union pour la Nouvelle République. Granted, even in the old days before General de Gaulle got onto East-West rapprochement, great masses of loyal party members defected in the polling booth and voted for him, even though opposed to all he stands for inside France and some of what he does outside—nuclear testing, for instance. They ponder how to make war on the only Western leader who has made personal peace with Moscow. This perplexity will not hurt the general on election day.

Looking ahead to the election there is some feeling . . . that the Gaullists are headed for a clean majority of their own in the 487-man Assembly, instead of the shared majority they hold now with the help of Valéry Giscard d'Estaing's Independent Republicans. But Jean Lecanuet, the surprisingly powerful vote-puller in the presidential elections last year, is bidding to bite out the center for himself, and François Mitterrand, the leftist who took 46 per cent of the vote in the runoff, is struggling hard to consolidate the left.

THE DEATH OF GAULLISM [6]

Charles de Gaulle was licked on December 5, 1965, and it was not just an ordinary trouncing. If an incumbent president gathers, on an election date of his own choice, only 45 per cent of the popular vote, the calamity is considered in any ordinary democracy pretty catastrophic. But in Charles de Gaulle's France, a veritable demo-monarchy, it was neoregicide. Of course, as the OAS [Organisation de l'Armée Secrète] (the terrorist organization that tried to prevent Algerian independence) found out again and again, de Gaulle is an accomplished escape artist. He always travels in the company of expendable substitutes. The expendable victim of December 5, 1965, was Gaullism; while the general, to no one's surprise, stayed alive long enough to be elected, two weeks later, President of France by the distressingly small majority of 5 per cent.

Gaullisme? C'est de Gaulle

But what makes an evaluation of the recent French whodunit particularly difficult is what has made any discussion of French affairs unmanageable for the last six years: there were no two people on earth who could agree on a definition of Gaullism. What, indeed, *was* that darned thing? A political philosophy? An ideology? A set of social and national aims? And *what* aims? These questions, and a hundred more, needed to be answered (and never were) before one could embark upon a sensible discussion of France's present and future. In several years of careful listening, I heard only one intelligent answer (from one of the General's most articulate aides): "Gaullisme? C'est de Gaulle."

So there were, after all, at least two people who agreed on a definition of Gaullism; and I am the third. But the rest of the

[6] From article by William S. Schlamm, author and political affairs analyst. *National Review.* 18:63-5. Ja. 25, '66. Reprinted by permission of *National Review,* 150 East 35th Street, New York, N.Y. 10016.

world kept insisting on a political rationale—and kept chasing the shadow of shadows ("the riddle wrapped in an enigma"). The truth is that Gaullism, just like Charles de Gaulle himself, was wholly and completely apolitical. The non-French universe, particularly around Washington, reverberated with speculations: whether de Gaulle "really" wanted an alliance with Germany or with the Soviet Union; whether he was "actually" for or against "Algérie Française"; whether he was . . . a Monarchist or a Democrat or a Fascist or a Communist; whether or not he hated America more than he feared the Soviet Union; whether he advocated or repudiated the unification of Europe. . . . The general does not give a damn one way or the other. He is constitutionally incapable of *any* political commitment. . . . He simply has no organ for evaluating political structures—and precisely because of this he was able to make use of *all* of them: his greatest strength was his total numbness in all matters of political judgment and decision. . . .

What, then, *was* Gaullism? Gaullism was Charles de Gaulle's notion that France needed a ruler—not just a government, not just political leadership, not even a dictator, but an honest-to-God ruler, a true king—in short, Charles de Gaulle. And this was indeed what France needed—in 1958, and for a few years more. The France that emerged in 1945 was perhaps the most defeated nation of Europe. France was sick to death. A ghastly cancer of defeatism had sucked the marrow from the nation's bones, and there was no social structure left fully alive in the country, not even communism. Such normal entities of national existence as Capital and Labor, the Upper Class and the Middle Class, were all in a state of atomization. Politics, in France, was nothing but frenzied catatonia. No social or political force could do more than keep all others from moving. And the decay reached its epitome, its spooky apotheosis, in Algeria.

In the case of Algeria there were of course, as there always are, two possibilities: either France would let Algeria go, or France would fight to keep her. So the French Left dreamed of letting Algeria go—but to capitulate would have meant to be hung by the French Right. And the French Right dreamed of fighting for "Algérie Française"—but to fight for Algeria would have meant civil war. Left and Right had finally stared each other into total immobility; and so France, evidently, needed a ruler. Only two structures were left in France with a modicum of cohesiveness—the Communist party and the army. The Communist party *had* a ruler; but he was also the ruler of the Soviet Union, and the Soviet Union, at that time, was not interested in a serious showdown in Western Europe. Which allowed the French army to call upon a ruler of its own choice. It was of course Charles de Gaulle.

His own invincible persuasion that he was born to rule France suited, in 1958, the French army's realization that France needed to be ruled. Charles de Gaulle, the creator as well as the creature of the French army, took the power from the army's outstretched palm—and used it against the army. He was installed to overcome the deadlock between the army and the Communist party, France's last cohesive structures. And then he went and decapitated the army. In 1959, it was not generally visible that, after the decimation of the French army, no other vital structure would remain in France than the Communist party. But some people saw it even then; and six years later, in December 1965, the whole world could see that the Front Populaire was getting ready to take over France.

What had happened since 1958? In seven years, the mighty and elated ruler had ruled so successfully that he was no longer needed. De Gaulle had worked himself out of his job: Gaullism is dead because Charles de Gaulle was such an unparalleled success.

France is again a healthy, normal and ordinary nation, pulsating with social energies, vibrant and prosperous. . . . National income, living standards, wages and profits, highways and construction, consumers' expenditures, capital investments, and savings have reached record heights. Of course, the general has not the slightest idea how all this happened: if there is anything Charles de Gaulle is constitutionally less capable of comprehending than politics, it is economics. But merely by sitting, even though illegitimately, on France's throne, merely by acting the ruler, Charles de Gaulle restored, for France, that indispensable "environment of confidence" without which no economy can grow or even exist. France, merely by looking up to an airily self-assured, haughty and inaccessible ruler, has in seven years overcome its national defeat—and has turned cocky again. The very first thing a cocky France did was to murder Gaullism.

For Charles de Gaulle . . . was not a real king. He ruled, not by the grace of God, but merely by the grace of a disheartened people which, when it felt its sap running again, also felt like firing the hired ruler. For the French, thank God, are an ornery and capricious people. De Gaulle's contract, to be sure, was finally renewed, by a measly 5 per cent margin [in the runoff election—Ed.], but it has changed in nature: Charles de Gaulle is no longer hired to rule France; he's merely employed again, with the humiliating job description of the "lesser evil." Better de Gaulle than the Front Populaire [in which, presumably, the Communists would have considerable, if not dominant, power —Ed.].

What happened was this. De Gaulle lost the election on December 5 [1965], but did not win the election of December 19—Mitterrand [de Gaulle's opponent] lost it. That's all. About two million Frenchmen who had voted against Charles de Gaulle on December 5 found themselves unable to vote for Mitterrand, the candidate of the Communist party [as well as the choice of various other anti-Gaullist groups—Ed.], two weeks later. Even so 45 out of 100 Frenchmen *did* vote for the greater evil; and only 55, though many of them have the gravest doubts about the general, preferred the devil to the deep red sea.

Captive of the Left

I, for one, find this result profoundly disturbing. Normally, the French Communist party receives about 23 per cent of the French vote, and the French Socialist party, another 14 per cent; but, combined on December 19, they gathered up 45 per cent instead of their "normal" 37 per cent. Even more, there is considerable evidence that, in addition to that frightening 45 per cent, hundreds of thousands of Front Populaire votes went to Charles de Gaulle this time—and for perfectly good reasons.

The general, to begin with, is at this moment rather indispensable to the Kremlin. The Soviets' European strategy is based on isolating Germany, on preventing her nuclear armament, on paralyzing NATO (and all other promises of European unification). Now, whether or not the general understands what he is doing, and whether or not he intends to continue doing it, his policies are holding back the growth of the Common Market, so understandably desired by Bonn, and have contributed to the undermining of NATO. Were de Gaulle to disappear these policies might change. Therefore, Moscow wanted Charles de Gaulle to stay—and the Soviet press, despite its commitment to the Front Populaire, was gentle, indeed, in its handling of de Gaulle. And, sure enough, a great many leftist luminaries in Paris rallied behind de Gaulle. *L'Express,* Jean-Jacques Servan-Schreiber's leftist newsweekly, estimates that only 65 per cent of the French workers—who usually vote Communist or Socialist—cast their ballots for Mitterrand on December 19. Between December 5 and December 19, the general was so desperately in search of support that he and his campaign managers openly courted Popular Front votes: he wanted to be, proclaimed de Gaulle, president of the Left as well as of everybody else. . . .

Moscow a Big Factor

And his foreign policy: He will continue his policy of not *having* a policy; and he will, with this very posture of unpredictable indifference to political commitment, profitably confuse the whole world (including, perhaps even the Soviets). Concepts like Democracy and Communism, Alliance and Friendship, Freedom and Independence, are meaningful to . . . ordinary people like you and me. They are not meaningful to Charles de Gaulle. He handles them as more or less useful and always interchangeable objects—meant only to be put together in a jigsaw puzzle designed to his own taste.

Only one thing is predictable: Charles de Gaulle will carefully avoid any political move that might provoke the Left to turn against him in earnest. If he is not careful, the Left can fire him. For the first time in his life, the general is running scared. He will cling to the leftist splinter that helped him cross the fateful 50 per cent mark on December 19—those elegant people who dream camp dreams of Europe from "the Atlantic to the Urals" and of the "enigmatic destiny of China." No one knows precisely how strong this group is, but the vote of December 19 is vaguely indicative: de Gaulle regained, compared to the vote of December 5, about 11 per cent. Where from? The disciplined radicals of the extreme Right . . . seem unanimously to have obeyed their leader's pretty silly directive to vote, second time around, for the candidate of the Front Populaire. (This bloc accounts for about 5 per cent.)

If this is so, then a leftist swing-group of about 10 per cent will determine the fate of France. The next national elections, in about a year, could break de Gaulle's power in a new Chamber of Deputies. Thus, during the next twelve months, de Gaulle will cater to that leftist swing-group. He will, perforce, have to pursue his "Atlantic to the Urals" policy no matter what the damage to the Common Market and the ideal of an eventual united Europe, in the sense of a politically federated Europe, and he will continue to chip away at United States dominance of NATO. Whether these operations will end up by torpedoing the Atlantic Community is uncertain; many responsible Western European statesmen and observers are pessimistic about what another two, five or seven years of de Gaulle in the Élysée will augur for Western Europe.

Subtracting the 37 per cent of the French voters who are irretrievably committed to the Front Populaire, the non-Communist and anti-Communist reservoir of the French electorate (about 60 per cent) would have to rally to the anti-Communist cause with an almost total dedication. Such a rally is not unthinkable—if a courageous leadership were determined to evoke it. But no such leadership is available in France as long as Charles de Gaulle retains even a formal franchise.

Now that Gaullism is dead, and France resumes its normal bourgeois existence without a lofty ruler, the tide of the Front

Populaire is rolling in. How fast and how far it will move, and how finally, depends not so much on the boldness of the Communist party, or on the conscience of the general, but on the strategic concerns of the Soviet Union. If Moscow, as seems likely, were to decide that it is still not interested in dramatic upheavals of the corrupt Western camp, then it may take a few more years before the French Communists enter the government. But should the stress of the revolutionary competition with Red China demand it, then Moscow will spur on its French party; in which case de Gaulle might die sooner than he thinks.

FRENCH CAUTIOUS ON RED COALITION [7]

"The Communist party is becoming respectable in France. But there still seem to be definite limits to the cooperation the Communists can achieve with other political parties."

Political experts . . . offer this comment on the chances for building a new "popular front" of leftist parties in time to affect France's 1967 parliamentary elections.

Five or six weeks ago the Communist Party and the so-called "Mitterrand federation" of non-Communist leftist parties were making very friendly bows in each other's direction. Since then both groups appear to have discovered reasons to slow down their reciprocal advances.

At first these were seen as leading toward a new "popular front" like that of 1930's. In those years Socialist Premier Léon Blum worked uneasily in partnership with the Communists led by Moscow-trained Maurice Thorez. Both leaders have now passed on.

An even closer grouping of parties seemed possible earlier this year.

François Mitterrand, the runner-up in the contest for the French presidency last December, stated publicly in June that Communists might have a role in some future French govern-

[7] From article by Carlyle Morgan, staff correspondent. *Christian Science Monitor.* p 1+. Jl. 25, '66. Reprinted by permission from *The Christian Science Monitor.* © 1966 The Christian Science Publishing Society. All rights reserved.

ment. They were not in the Blum government. A cabinet role in future would, of course, depend on the leftist parties continuing to win political victories with Communist aid.

Guarded Attitude

Waldeck Rochet, leader of the French Communist party, responded to Mr. Mitterrand favorably. He also spoke of a Communist role in government. . . .

Since then the attitude of the Communists to the Mitterrand overture has appeared more guarded. And on its side the federation has been facing political facts that may limit cooperation in a common front.

The Communists show themselves as aiming to maintain their own separateness from other parties. They do this even while using teamwork with non-Communist parties in an effort to make communism a leading factor in French political life.

The party central committee has published its own generalized program for the election. It has also said in effect that it likes the Mitterrand federation program. But it has not followed this comment with a proposal that the two groups get together to form a common program.

On its side the federation speaks as if it regarded its program as a common one. Yet its leaders also hedge.

Cooperation Needed

One of the hedgers is Guy Mollet. He is secretary-general of the Socialist party. This party is the the heart of the federation.

Mr. Mollet has pointed out that the federation sent its program to the Communist party. But he added that the federation meant only to "inform" the French Communist leaders.

This statement aimed to prevent charges that the federation was ready to permit the Communists to help share its program.

This is necessary because it could lose much voter support if it is too closely allied with the Communists.

One of the three elements of the leftist federation along with Socialists and the newer "political clubs" is the Radical Socialist party.

Radical candidates, who are really middle roaders, will need the cooperation of the even more conservative Popular Republican Movement (MRP) in some localities.

This would consist of agreements to let strong candidates from either party run in the second round of voting while those who made weak showings in the first round would stand aside.

The MRP is led by Senator Jean Lecanuet who was third man in the December presidential election. He took important votes away from the Gaullists among Roman Catholics and conservatives. But he could not have taken any Communist votes from the left.

The Communists have warned that they would not tolerate a very close partnership between themselves and the federation if some federation members were to seek allies among Senator Lecanuet's followers.

Major Differences

Obviously the strategic background is complex. As for programs, there are both similarities and differences in federation and Communist points of view.

One major difference appears over foreign policy. The federation favors the Atlantic alliance. The Communists are against it.

Both the federation and the Communists are opposing the Gaullists in parliament. But the Communists favor General de Gaulle's attack on NATO, while the federation opposes his action.

The French Communists demand not only "suppression of NATO" but also of the Warsaw Pact. This position is also close to General de Gaulle's.

In the related field of defense, both the federation and the Communists are against the Gaullist nuclear *force de frappe.* Also they both oppose nuclear-weapons tests by France such as those which have . . . taken place in the South Pacific.

They both favor the nuclear test ban which the United States and the Soviet Union have signed. They demand that France join this test ban.

They both favor disarmament efforts such as those at Geneva which are aiming at a complete test ban and a treaty against the spread of nuclear weapons. They believe France should be taking a full part in the Geneva [disarmament] talks instead of standing aloof, on General de Gaulle's order.

Bridging Effort

In domestic affairs the federation program has tried to bridge positions between the two groups. It comes out for nationalization of large industries. But the Communists are unappreciative. They say the federation does not go far enough on nationalization.

The Communist program demands specifically the nationalization of "steel and iron industries and iron ore mines, chemicals, oil, automobile manufacture, electronics, aircraft builders, air transport, big banks, and insurance companies."

The Communists also say the federation is not strong enough in its demands for higher wages and more benefits for workers. They accuse the federation of being "vague" on these matters.

On the question of the "presidential power" the federation likewise fails to please the Communists completely. Both groups want to curb this power which they say General de Gaulle wields as "personal rule." But the Communists complain that the federation does not "spell out" how to end personal rule.

Vague Programs

The Communists urge repeal of the constitutional article that gives special powers to the president. The federation has not clearly said it would repeal this article, according to some of its critics.

While the Communists accuse the federation of being vague, experienced, impartial political experts at Paris say both programs are vague.

These experts point out, moreover, that the Communists do not seem to be trying to define issues clearly enough to negotiate with the federation for a popular front. For this reason, most seasoned observers here seem to agree that the Communists are not pressing from their side for a popular front as this was understood in the 1930's.

French Communist leaders say that "times have changed" and that "history does not repeat itself." This is their comment on the prospect for a "popular front."

One reason they show this independence is that they know how great is the need of the non-Communist leftist parties for their aid.

The Communist party is still the biggest party in France. It pulls in 20 per cent or better of the French vote. It is the only thoroughly organized party. It is supported by hard workers who go out and get signatures for its petitions.

INDIVIDUALISM GROWS YOUNGER [8]

"Patriotism is not enough for me."

"Does God exist?"

"I feel I must seek satisfaction in learning how to serve the needs of others."

"I am not sure I want to be a Christian."

"We must learn to cooperate—to work in groups."

All kinds of questions. All kinds of answers.

Which is the way it would have to be in this diverse land of France.

France, the humorist Pierre Daninos said some years ago, is a nation divided by 43 million Frenchmen. The population has increased since then. Today he might say that France is a nation divided by 48 million individualists.

But one third of the population—16 million—are people less than twenty years old. And this would mix up the Daninos

[8] From article by Carlyle Morgan, staff correspondent. *Christian Science Monitor.* p 1. Jl. 5, '66. Reprinted by permission from *The Christian Science Monitor.* © 1966 The Christian Science Publishing Society. All rights reserved.

arithmetic. For among the young 16 million are many thousands who hold ideas about cooperation which would have astonished the generation that went before them.

If these ideas continue to develop, they could transform French life, which hitherto has accented individualism.

Indeed as never before the actions and thoughts of France's young people are shaping the nation's future.

Youthful Influence Marked

Young people are specially influential in today's France because of their numbers, and because of the amount of money they control; for example five or six million teenagers spend about $2 billion a year.

More of these young people are urgently seeking self-development—mental and moral—than anyone might guess from the statistics on sales of luxury products to young people.

The foreign observer in France today will not see where the nation is heading just by following the course of a sports car roaring through the traffic of Paris's Place de la Concorde.

The cars, motor scooters, musical instruments, radios, television sets, sporting goods, or clothing young people buy and the entertainment they seek create much-publicized "image."

Young people's tastes become more and more decisive for manufacturers, marketing, and advertising. What has already happened in the United States is happening here. France is becoming a country not only of, but for, young people.

But at the same time studies of French youth are showing that the newer generation is thinking about a lot of things other than luxuries. It is asking about God, religion, nationalism.

Young people here show less and less interest in joining the traditional political parties. They want no part of old ideological quarrels that have divided French political life for centuries.

Even Gaullism does not seem attractive to French young people. One of President de Gaulle's most fervent admirers—the renowned author François Mauriac—has noted this lack of interest. A surprising number of them cannot put country first in the sense that Gaullism does.

Travel Fostered

French students more and more are using vacations to study in other countries. They are encouraged in such interests by employer groups, farm organizations, junior chambers of commerce.

A government secretariat fosters foreign travel. It arranges low-cost trips, offers travel grants, and welcomes young people from other countries to France. The French-German Treaty of 1963 has led to the setting up of a French-German Youth Office, which helps develop friendship between the youth of the two countries.

More than fifty French organizations are planning foreign educational trips for young people today. Nine organizations promote work programs which bring young people of all nationalities together in France or abroad, including Africa.

Young people here do not feel that even large alliances are a broad enough framework for their loyalty. They think in world terms.

In this idealism many older people will think they recognize themselves when young. The idealism may be partly due to inexperience.

But the fervor comes also from a new world environment. Developments in transportation, communication, and even possibility of annihilation have intensified a sense of urgency in young people's search for useful activity.

FOUR VIEWS ON SEVEN YEARS [9]

Whatever he achieves or fails to achieve in the future, Charles de Gaulle has already left a permanent mark on French history —and not all Frenchmen are convinced that it has been a completely beneficial one. For an appraisal of de Gaulle's first seven years as president, *Newsweek* turned to four eminent Frenchmen of widely varied political opinions. Their verdicts:

[9] From article in *Newsweek*. 66:44-5. D. 13, '65. Copyright, Newsweek, Inc., December, 1965. Reprinted by permission.

Raymond Aron, writer and columnist

In three respects de Gaulle's return to power has proved a good thing for France: he introduced the notion of governmental stability, he carried out the much-needed devaluation of the franc [in 1958] and he put an end to the Algerian war. Probably only de Gaulle could have granted Algeria independence without shattering the fabric of France itself. Any other Frenchman would certainly have been branded as a traitor, and it's to de Gaulle's lasting credit that he acted as he did, and that the process occurred without civil war in France.

As I see them, the limitations of General de Gaulle's policies are these: first, he has elaborated a constitution which is tailor-made for himself but which—in the absence of de Gaulle—may easily prove as unworkable as France's previous constitutions. When de Gaulle has disappeared from the political scene, it is unlikely that Parliament will accept remaining fettered the way it is now, for the power of General de Gaulle is not only due to the constitution but to his prestige and influence.

Secondly, the foreign policy of Charles de Gaulle is, of course, superb theater. But in the final analysis, it has not had a decisive impact on problems or events. As far as Europe is concerned, one should remember that General de Gaulle doesn't regard the pursuit of a high standard of living as a worthy end in itself. West Germany may be more prosperous, with a greater industrial capacity, and represent more economic potential in the world than does France, but it is still, as de Gaulle sees it, a country cut in two, dependent on the United States for the defense of Berlin. In other words, it is not an independent country, and for de Gaulle independence—or rather, nondependence on others—is the real goal of any diplomacy.

As far as the European Community and NATO are concerned, de Gaulle has not taken the irrevocable step of breaking with these institutions. But if he hasn't actually destroyed the Common Market he has seriously affected its image, and broken its charm. Unless de Gaulle leaves the political scene very soon indeed, my feeling is that the concept of a politically united

Europe is dead—and de Gaulle will have played a big part in bringing this about.

Emmanuel d'Astier de La Vigerie, former interior minister

General de Gaulle has been blamed for shortcomings in France's educational and social fields. But surely it is significant that of approximately 4 million Communist voters in France, about a million of them will vote for de Gaulle. This leads me to think, whatever statistics may say, that French workers are not so downtrodden as some anti-Gaullists would have one believe. It is difficult to evaluate the happiness of a nation, but, at a guess, I would say there is no doubt that French workers have had a better time under de Gaulle than they did from 1947 to 1958.

As far as General de Gaulle's broader policies are concerned, he is accused frequently of being anti-European and pro-Communist. He is said to wield personal power and to ignore the eventuality of his own demise, which would plunge France into chaos.

Such accusations miss the point. In de Gaulle's philosophy, parliamentary democracy is dead or dying, and not only in France. In de Gaulle's view all modern power is becoming personalized. Ideologies everywhere now count less than results. The world has become a more pragmatic place. It has changed in other respects as well. The Soviet Union has become a wealthy industrialized power; the Communist menace—in the wealthy, industrialized countries—is fading and we are faced instead with the revolt of the have-nots in the underdeveloped countries. De Gaulle's free, independent foreign policy does not stem from opportunism but from a vital concern for the future as he sees it—and the need to avoid a clash between the "haves" and the "have-nots." He does not feel that the United States has a solution to this problem.

Of course, there's the danger of chaos in France after de Gaulle, but that is no reason for ushering back chaos now. The chances of chaos will recede as time goes on. And if—as is the case, I think—personal power is here to stay, let's at least be ruled by a man of genius.

Pierre Uri, economist

General de Gaulle is an extraordinarily skilled actor, and his performance has attracted immense attention. But pageantry and publicity apart, what are the lasting results of General de Gaulle's policy? Has France played a decisive role in any of the major crises in our time? The answer is an unequivocal no.

In a series of spectacular gestures, General de Gaulle has pandered to the nationalism inherent in many Frenchmen still. But the only way France could have played a decisive role in the world was by acting in concert with the [Common Market] Six, by pressing for a cohesive common "European" attitude to a given problem. Instead, General de Gaulle has been intent on minimizing the importance and scope of Europe.

On the home front, General de Gaulle has had at his disposal almost absolute powers for seven years. The results are disappointing. Economically, the parallel of the Eisenhower Administration comes to mind: an orthodox, ultraconservative policy leading to stagnation. France's deflationary policy has pegged prices, and by juggling figures, much has been made of "balancing the budget," whatever that may mean. But this same deflationary policy has slowed down the pace of capital investment to such a degree that France is rapidly being outdistanced by West Germany: two years ago West Germany had 50 per cent more productive capacity than France. Today it has 75 per cent more capacity.

Partly, these failures are due to a lack of parliamentary control. The main vice of the Fourth Republic was too much parliamentary control, which caused governmental instability. But the Fifth Republic has gone to the opposite extreme and has none.

The real key to General de Gaulle is that he is a born gambler. He doesn't really know what he wants but is prepared to gamble in order to go as far, in any direction, as he can. And he is so deliberately secretive that he is always able to claim, after the event, that what he obtained in the last resort was what he wanted in the first place.

Paul Reynaud, a former French premier [who died in 1966]

I approved of General de Gaulle's policy toward Algeria. But I cannot approve of his present foreign policy. Indeed, I feel that France should, for her own good, change this policy now, while there is still time to change it. For de Gaulle, who is certainly not consciously pro-Communist, is pursuing a course which is primarily beneficial only to the Soviet Union; he is weakening the NATO alliance and destroying the fabric of a united Europe.

The Soviet Union is also interested in doing away with NATO, and doesn't want a powerful, united Europe. In "going it alone" without our allies, without Europe, and in deliberately destroying the ancient and valued friendship of the United States, de Gaulle has thrown away his real chance of greatness. This consisted in following in the path laid down by the late Robert Schuman, France's foreign minister who helped establish both the European Coal and Steel Community and the Common Market. If de Gaulle had not upset the work of Schuman, the general could have become the first president of the United States of Europe.

It is difficult to find a positive element in any of de Gaulle's foreign-policy gestures. He has successively turned to West Germany, to the Soviet Union and to China in an attempt to play a major role on the world scene, and in each case he has failed.

As far as de Gaulle's home policy is concerned, I feel that France is not devoting enough of her resources to productive investment, and this may seriously weaken us as a European power in a year or two. General de Gaulle, so intent on the judgment of history, may find to his surprise that his stock may not stand as high with future historians as he expects.

II. DE GAULLE SPEAKS

EDITOR'S INTRODUCTION

For de Gaulle, language is not merely a method of expression. It is a form of art and a tool to be used in shaping works of beauty and meaning. So it is that when de Gaulle speaks or writes, his words have a regal tone, a measured cadence. Nor does de Gaulle use words lightly. Everything he says has been carefully considered and polished to a high sheen.

This makes it almost obligatory that a book on France under the rule of de Gaulle contain a selection of his addresses and statements—all the more so because the French president has no better interpreter than himself. Even a cursory reading of some of de Gaulle's writings reveals a remarkable consistency of thought and a single-mindedness of aim. For instance, de Gaulle's withdrawal from NATO's integrated command structure in 1966 was the logical result of what he had been saying and doing for some years back. His determination to prevent any European political integration could also have been foretold by careful attention to his early statements. And though the Western world was shocked when de Gaulle vetoed the British Common Market application bid in 1963, it need not have been, because the veto was a predictable corollary of what de Gaulle had long been saying.

This section offers a selection of de Gaulle's addresses, statements, and press conferences over the years. The first piece gives his interpretation of modern French history. The next selection, taken from a 1960 press conference, contains the seeds of decay of the Atlantic alliance. Subsequent selections cover a wide variety of subjects: the reasons for the veto of the British Common Market bid; de Gaulle's view of French relations with the low-income countries in Africa, Asia, and Latin America; his concept of national independence; his views on Franco-Russian cooperation and his most recent thoughts on Vietnam and Germany. Singly, these pieces help explain why de Gaulle has done what he has done. Together, they add up to a broad view of French policy during the 1960's.

ON FRANCE [1]

Once upon a time there was an old country all hemmed in by habits and circumspection. At one time the richest, the mightiest people among those in the center of the world stage, after great misfortunes it came, as it were, to withdraw within itself. While other peoples were growing around it, it remained immobile. In an era when the power of states depended upon their industrial might, the great sources of power were stingily meted out to it. It had little coal. It had no petroleum. Furthermore, its population was no longer growing as, in some years, it numbered fewer births than deaths. In the doubt and the bitterness which it came to have about itself as a result of this situation, political, social and religious struggles did not cease to divide it. Finally, after two world wars had decimated, ruined and torn it, many in the world were wondering whether it would succeed in getting back on its feet.

Now, this country, France, is back on her feet again. Already a national movement, which was embodied in the Resistance, had shown a determined will for renewal. Immediately following the Liberation, a great impulse was given. Afterwards, in spite of many rough stretches, the trend did not cease to turn toward expansion. But the difficult aftermath of a stagnant past continued to bear down upon the nation. Above all, the inconsistency of the state, whatever might have been the worth of individual men, condemned the constituted authorities always to be in a precarious position and always to be contested. Two years ago, we suddenly found ourselves on the brink of civil war. Doubtless, the occasion of this crisis was the Algerian question, which followed upon the humiliating outcome in Indochina, and

[1] From "Address by President Charles de Gaulle on French, African and Algerian Realities, Broadcast over French Radio and Television on June 14, 1960." Text from *Major Addresses, Statements and Press Conferences of General Charles de Gaulle, May 19, 1958-January 31, 1964.* French Embassy. 972 5th Ave. New York 10021. p 79-81.

called for new action. But, at the same time, we found ourselves, in our territories of Black Africa, in the presence of a great movement which was stirring that continent. Finally, and as everything is interrelated, the halting of foreign trade, the exhaustion of our credit, the ruin of our currency—all consequences of an inflation that [it] had been impossible to stem—were threatening, from one moment to the next, to hurl us into the abyss. That is when the country recognized the necessity of a great and strong policy.

It was necessary, at the very beginning, to insure the life of the nation by establishing a firm and stable basis for production, trade, the finances, the currency, the standard of living. I know that this calling a halt to the habit of taking the easiest way out—I know what this cost in terms of sacrifices, especially to Frenchmen in modest circumstances. At present, the country's economic activity is picking up again under healthier conditions. On the other hand, in Black Africa and in Madagascar, the institution of the Community [see "The French Community—Does It Exist?" in Section III, below] has opened up a reasonable channel for an impetus which, otherwise, might have led to the worst disruptions. In Algeria, France's decision—until then paralyzed by opposing prejudices and wishful thinking—was taken and proclaimed. As a result of this coherent body of political resolutions and of the exemplary confidence of which the whole French people have given proof, the entire world has recognized that order and progress have once again found their opportunity in our country.

But to accomplish what? To accomplish a great deal. For our purpose is to transform our old France into a new country and to enable her to fall in step with her time. From this policy, she must draw prosperity, power and world-wide influence. This change must be our great national ambition.

Since we are the French people, we must accede to the rank of a great industrial state or be resigned to our decline. Our choice is made. Our development is under way. Its aim is both the progress of French power and that of the human condition.

Our plans provide that it will be accomplished, in the next few years, at a rate of 5 per cent or 6 per cent a year, raising the average purchasing power by 4 per cent annually. This means that, in twenty years, France—short of a catastrophe—will be twice as prosperous as she is today. This also means that a young couple, to whom a child is born this morning, has every chance that their small son, when it is his turn to be a father, will find himself twice as well off as his parents are today. What is more, it may readily be supposed that the Common Market of the Six is hastening this development. But the fact that we are living in the industrial era does not keep agriculture from remaining an essential branch of France's economic life. Since we have the advantage of being able to feed ourselves from the products of our soil, since we have all that is needed to be the country of fine wheat, choice meat, pure milk, good wine, we will not allow this great economic, social and national potential to be exhausted.

Women and men of France, you can see with your own eyes what is being done for France. Naturally, first of all, we are bending our efforts to give her the sources of power that she lacks. The point we have reached proves that our efforts were justified: coal in plentiful supply; French or African petroleum, which in five years will cover our needs; gas from Lacq which, little by little, is being distributed; soon, gas from the Sahara, whose inexhaustible reserves may transform the existence of Algeria and influence that of Europe; electricity produced by hydroelectric power in quantities twice as large as those which were produced ten years ago; atomic energy which model installations have begun to supply. This accession of France to the rank of a people, which will find within its boundaries energy, electricity, oil and gas, and will furnish them to others, is one of the most striking facts of world evolution, which, from the point of view of our independence, will have immeasurable consequences.

On condition, of course, that our country is at the same time given the necessary equipment. I will certainly not assert that all is for the best in this respect. However, look at what changes are being made, day after day, in France's industrial plant; what an effort is constantly being exerted to reconvert it; what a proportion of the profits are being reinvested with a view to development; what an improvement there is in the social atmosphere of our corporations, while awaiting the association of workers in the enterprises. And, in agriculture, the reorganization of the whole structure, of production, of equipment, of marketing and purchasing—a movement which alone can raise agriculture to the level of realities and which will increase under the impetus of law. Finally, note the rate of transformation of our infrastructure: the highway system, railroads, ports, airports and water supply. There is not a traveler, a tourist, a camper who does not notice this from season to season.

But what would this development of material resources amount to, were it not coupled with the development of human resources? Now, we know that the French birth rate has made a striking comeback, that there are nearly 300,000 more cradles than graves a year and that this human investment will have a powerful influence on the country's economy. What social insurance is providing in the way of security for Frenchmen, and thereby for our economy, is well known. It is also well known that 300,000 dwelling units are being built each year and that this contributes directly to the productivity of the national labor force. It is well known what strides are being made in the country's hospitals, and to what an extent suffering and anxiety are relieved thereby, to the benefit of the whole community. But it is also and especially well known what a tremendous transformation is being achieved in education. While, I must note, the law is trying to organize cooperation between public and private institutions, we intend to give all our youth a level of knowledge commensurate with modern times, to enlarge the field from which the nation's activity draws the values which are necessary to it and to give to each child every chance at the beginning of his life in the community. As facts and figures are more eloquent than words, I shall state, for example, that secondary education will soon enroll 3 million students, or fifteen times as many as at the beginning of the century, and that our universities will enroll, in the next ten years, 600,000 students, whereas only 30,000 were registered in 1900.

In truth, in order to have an idea what an enormous burden the French nation is imposing upon its present gains with a view to building the future, one need only consider the use of public funds. Out of the entire state budget, while barely one fourth is absorbed by the functioning of the administrative services and another fourth goes for defense, the remainder, or half, is assigned to the material and human investments which all go, in the long run, to the national and social development of France.

ON THE ATLANTIC ALLIANCE [2]

Question: General de Gaulle, . . . can you throw some light on your concept of cooperation within NATO, which you have asked to have reformed?

Answer: It is more than ten years since the Atlantic alliance was organized in its present form. At that time, as I remember, the burning question, the immediate question, was merely the security of Europe. So we made an alliance limited to Europe, and one with a very narrow field of action. And furthermore, at that same time it appeared that the United States alone had the means for defense and that the states of Western Europe, of continental Europe at least, found themselves in a political, economic and social position, of which the best that can be said was that it was uncertain. Moreover, these states postponed the revival of their personality in the international sphere until a much later date, if they did not renounce it altogether. So the alliance was set up on the basis of integration, that is to say, of a system whereby the defense of each of the countries of continental Europe, of Western Europe—not counting England—does not have a national character; a system in which, in fact, everything is under the command of the Americans and in which the Americans decide on the use of the principal weapons, in other words, the atomic weapons.

[2] From "President Charles de Gaulle's Press Conferences (Excerpts): Third Press Conference, September 5, 1960." Text from *Atlantic Alliance: Allied Comment*. U.S. Congress. Senate. Committee on Government Operations. Supt. of Docs. Washington, D.C. 20402. '66. p 35-6.

But during the past ten years, much has changed. First of all, it became evident that the possibilities of conflict, and consequently of military operations, were spreading far beyond Europe, were spreading all over the world. It became evident that the Middle East and Africa, in particular, were danger spots quite as much as Europe and that there existed, between the principal members of the Atlantic alliance, political differences concerning them which, if the occasion arose, might turn into disagreements on strategy. Then, too, the countries of continental Europe, France in particular—we may be allowed to say so—regained their balance and began to prosper once more, and consequently as this occurred they regained awareness of themselves, especially where their defense was concerned. Finally one of them—you know which one [France]—began to build an atomic arsenal of its own. Now under these circumstances, France considers that what was done ten years ago within this limited field and on the single, exclusive basis of integration must be brought up to date. I shall naturally speak only of the points in which France is directly interested. As for the other countries, if one day there is a general confrontation, they will speak for themselves.

With regard to France, there are at least two points on which the treaty must be revised. Moreover, you know that when the treaty of the North Atlantic organization was drawn up, its text specified that it could be revised at the end of ten years, and the ten years have elapsed.

What are the two essential points for France? The first, as I have indicated, is the limitation of the alliance to the single area of Europe. We feel that, at least among the world powers of the West, there must be something organized—where the alliance is concerned—as to their political conduct and, should the occasion arise, their strategic conduct outside Europe, especially in the Middle East, and in Africa, where these three powers [the United States, Britain, and France] are constantly involved. Furthermore, if there is no agreement among the principal members of the Atlantic alliance on matters other than Europe, how can the alliance be indefinitely maintained in Europe? This must be remedied.

The second point on which France thinks there should be a change is that of integration in the defense of Europe. It seems to us that the defense of a country, while being of course combined with that of other countries, must have a national character. How indeed in the long run could a government, a parliament, a people give their money and their services with all their heart in time of peace, and make their sacrifices in time of war, for a system in which they are not responsible for their own defense? That is why from this point of view as well, a revision of the alliance seems indispensable to us. Moreover, as you know, we have already taken a few steps in this direction. That is why, for example, France keeps her fleet directly under her own orders. For exactly what is a fleet? It is a means of distant action. And how could it be imagined that France would leave this means of distant action to the discretion of an exclusively European organization which has nothing to do with Africa, while she herself, through her interests and her responsibilities, is continually involved in Africa?

Furthermore, France feels that if atomic weapons are to be stockpiled on her territory, these weapons should be in her own hands. Given the nature of these weapons and the possible consequences of their use, France obviously cannot leave her own destiny and even her own life to the discretion of others.

This is what France understands by the reform of the Atlantic organization, while repeating that there is certainly no question, of course, of separating from each other, for never has the Atlantic alliance met such a great need.

ON VETOING THE BRITISH COMMON MARKET APPLICATION BID [3]

Question: Can you explicitly define France's position concerning the entry of Britain in the Common Market and the political evolution of Europe?

[3] From President de Gaulle's "Seventh Press Conference, January 14, 1963: The Common Market." Text from *Atlantic Alliance: Allied Comment.* U.S. Congress. Senate. Comittee on Government Operations. Supt. of Docs. Washington, D.C. 20402. '66. p 38-40.

Answer: That is a clear question which I am going to try to answer clearly.

When we talk about economic matters, and even more when we are dealing with them, it is essential for what is said and what is done to conform to reality, for otherwise we end up in deadlocks and sometimes even ruined.

Concerning this very important question of the European Economic Community and also that of the possible membership of Great Britain, it is the facts which must be considered first. Sentiments, as favorable as they might be and as they are, cannot be put forward in opposition to the real factors of the problem. What are these factors?

The Treaty of Rome [the official name for the treaty which created the Common Market] was concluded between six continental states, states which are, in short, economically of the same nature. Whether in terms of their industrial or agricultural production, of their foreign trade, of their commercial customs and clients, or of their living and working conditions, there are many more similarities than differences between them. Moreover, they are adjacent, they interpenetrate, they are extensions of each other through their communications. The very fact of grouping them and linking them together in such a way that what they produce, buy, sell and consume they produce, buy, sell and consume by preference within their own grouping thus conforms to reality.

It must be added, moreover, that from the standpoint of their economic development, their social progress and their technological capability they are, in short, in stride with each other and they are moving forward at more or less the same pace. Furthermore, it happens that there exists between them no kind of political grievance, no border disputes, no rivalry for domination or power. To the contrary, there is a feeling of solidarity between them, firstly owing to the awareness they have of together possessing an important part of the origins of our civilization, and also with regard to their security, because they are continental countries and they are confronted by the same single threat from one end of their territorial grouping to the other.

Finally, they have a feeling of solidarity because not one of them is linked on the outside by any special political or military agreement.

Thus it has been psychologically and materially possible to organize an economic community of the Six. Moreover, this was not without difficulty. When the Treaty of Rome was signed in 1957, it was after long discussions, and once concluded, so that something could be accomplished, it was necessary for us French to straighten ourselves out in the economic, financial and monetary domain. And this was done in 1959.

From that time on, the Community was workable in principle, but it was then necessary to implement the Treaty. Now this Treaty, which was quite specific and complete on the subject of industry, was not at all specific and complete on the subject of agriculture. And yet, it was essential for our country that this be settled.

For it is indeed quite obvious that agriculture is an essential element of our national activity as a whole. We cannot conceive of a Common Market in which French agriculture would not find outlets commensurate with its production, and we agree, moreover, that, among the Six, we are the country for which this necessity is the most imperative.

That is why, . . . when consideration was being given to implementing the second stage of the Treaty, in other words, to a practical beginning of application, we were led to set the entry of agriculture into the Common Market as a formal condition.

This was finally accepted by our partners, but very complex and difficult arrangements were needed. And some of these arrangements are still being worked out. I will note in passing that, in this vast undertaking, all the decisions taken were taken by the governments, for nowhere else is there any authority or responsibility. But I should say that, in order to prepare and clarify matters, the Brussels Commission [charged with developing a Common Market agricultural policy] worked in a highly objective and pertinent fashion.

Then Great Britain applied for membership in the Common Market. It did so after refusing earlier to participate in the community that was being built, and after then having created a free trade area with six other states, and finally—I can say this, the negotiations conducted for so long on this subject can be recalled—after having put some pressure on the Six in order to prevent the application of the Common Market from really getting started. Britain thus in its turn requested membership, but on its own conditions.

This undoubtedly raises for each of the six states and for England problems of a very great dimension.

England is, in effect, insular, maritime, linked through its trade, markets and food supply to very diverse and often very distant countries. Its activities are essentially industrial and commercial, and only slightly agricultural. It has, throughout its work, very marked and original customs and traditions. In short, the nature, structure and economic context of England differ profoundly from those of the other states of the Continent.

What is to be done so that Britain, such as it lives, such as it produces and such as it trades, be incorporated into the Common Market such as it has been conceived and such as it functions?

For example, the means by which the people of Great Britain nourish themselves is in fact by importing foodstuffs purchased at low prices in the two Americas or in the former dominions, while still granting large subsidies to British farmers. This means is obviously incompatible with the system the Six have quite naturally set up for themselves.

The system of the Six consists of making a pool of the agricultural products of the entire Community, of strictly determining their prices, of forbidding subsidizing, of organizing their consumption between all the members and of making it obligatory for each of these members to pay to the Community any savings they might make by having foodstuffs brought in from outside instead of consuming those offered by the Common Market.

Once again, what is to be done to make Britain, such as it is, enter that system?

One was sometimes led to believe that our British friends, in applying for membership in the Common Market, agreed to change their own ways even to the point of applying all the conditions accepted and practiced by the Six, but, the question is to know if Great Britain can at present place itself, with the Continent and like it, within a tariff that is truly common, give up all preference with regard to the Commonwealth, cease to claim that its agriculture be privileged and, even more, consider as null and void the commitments it has made with the countries that are part of its free trade area. That question is the one at issue.

One cannot say that it has now been resolved. Will it be so one day? Obviously Britain alone can answer that.

The question is raised all the more since, following Britain, other states . . . would or will want to enter the Common Market.

It must be agreed that the entry first of Great Britain and then that of those other states will completely change the series of adjustments, agreements, compensations and regulations already established between the Six, because all these states, like Britain, have very important traits of their own. We would then have to envisage the construction of another Common Market. But the eleven-member, then thirteen-member and then perhaps eighteen-member Common Market that would be built would, without any doubt, hardly resemble the one the Six have built.

Moreover, this Community, growing in that way, would be confronted with all the problems of its economic relations with a crowd of other states, and first of all with the United States.

It is foreseeable that the cohesion of all its members, who would be very numerous and very diverse, would not hold for long and that in the end there would appear a colossal Atlantic Community under American dependence and leadership which would soon completely swallow up the European Community.

This is an assumption that can be perfectly justified in the eyes of some, but it is not at all what France wanted to do and what France is doing, which is a strictly European construction.

Then, it is possible that Britain would one day come round to transforming itself enough to belong to the European Community without restriction and without reservation, and placing it ahead of anything else, and in that case the Six would open the door to it and France would place no obstacle in its path, although obviously the mere membership of Britain in the Community would completely change its nature and its volume.

ON LATIN AMERICA AND THE
DEVELOPING COUNTRIES [4]

Question: What place could Latin America have in your policy of cooperation with the developing countries?

Answer: It is quite true that the development of the countries of the world, and in particular of those which, up to now, have just made a start on this great movement, is the world question par excellence. There is a modern civilization. Europe invented it and then transported it to America. Today the West, on both sides of the Atlantic, remains the source and the artisan of this civilization. To combine the labor of man with the output of machines—that is what this immense effort of progress consists of. Science, technology and politics play essential roles in this.

Now, this civilization has reached the rest of the world where the peoples, who practiced other and sometimes very advanced civilizations, are turning toward the new one. So long as natural obstacles, distance, hostility and immobilism held these faraway masses apart from the new currents, the developed countries could only see the lagging countries as exotic markets or lands to colonize. Between the two, contacts were hardly established except by the explorers, traders, soldiers, missionaries or administrators whom the former sent to the latter. But this era has come to an end.

Through the effect of communications, the military, political and economic interpenetration which occurred during the two world wars, the movement of idealism which, on the part of the most advanced, determined many minds to want to assist those

[4] From President de Gaulle's press conference, January 31, 1964. Text from *Major Addresses, Statements and Press Conferences of General Charles de Gaulle, May 19, 1958-January 31, 1964.* French Embassy. 972 5th Ave. New York 10021. p 250-2.

less provided for, those countries are gradually becoming aware of all they lack. Of course, the rivalry of the totalitarian camp and that of liberty, as well as the national ambitions which are at work under the cover of ideologies, do not fail to cause, in this vast change, ferments of all sorts. But, whatever the case, two billion men today aspire to progress, a better life and dignity. Since the world has existed, this is a fact whose importance and scope have never been equaled.

Naturally France, despite the ordeals which for a time were able to hurt and weaken her, plays a considerable role in this vast evolution. This is undoubtedly due to the positions which her policy, her economy, her culture and her strength have acquired for her in all parts of the world. But this is also and especially due to the nature of her genius which has made her, at all times, a ferment and a champion of human liberation. Despite the jolts to our action in this area, we have always returned to our general line. Besides the countless actions and encouragements which we have lavished, over the centuries, to assist the emancipation of oppressed peoples or men, and besides the spiritual and cultural influences which, starting in our country, are spreading in the same direction in all parts of the world, the mark of what we gave to others to raise their condition, in all places where we found ourselves, is blazingly engraved on many souls and on many soils. Certainly, at the time when colonization was the only path which made it possible to penetrate peoples folded up in their sleep, we were colonizers and at times imperious and harsh. But, in sum, what we have accomplished as such leaves a largely positive balance in the nations in which we have done it.

However, the evolution long under way from one end of the world to the other and the world-wide upset caused by the world wars made decolonization inescapable. Moreover, the Western powers, by spreading among the peoples they administered, particularly among the elites, the ideas and the practice of their own civilization, themselves prepared for the emancipation of the colonized peoples. . . . To grant all the peoples who were not actually our own but who were dependent on us the right of self-determination, to conduct the affair in such a way that in the final analysis and despite wrenches this was done in agreement with us and that then, in friendship, fine and fruitful cooperation was established between us and the new states—this was in fact the policy of France. . . .

It is, quite naturally, to the overseas nations which, starting from our administration, have become sovereign states, that we are above all lending our aid. Of course, this is costly for us. An important report has recently been submitted . . . with regard to all the aspects of this aid, wherever supplied. Public aid— that is, the aid furnished from one state to another, in economic, financial, technological, cultural and military areas—amounts to about $1 billion a year. As for the many forms of private aid, it amounts to some $400 million. The $1.4 billion that we thus draw annually from our resources are equivalent to more than 2 per cent of our national revenue and more than 10 per cent of the investments we make in France. There is not a single nation in the world that dedicates to the progress of others a similar proportion of what it is doing for its own. After us, the next, from this point of view, is America. Doubtless America offers a great number of countries various forms of aid whose total, in absolute value, is much larger, but in relation to its means, the aid America furnishes is not, in percentages, half of our own. As for the Soviet Union, it is still much farther behind.

It is true that this cooperation is not only a one-way affair. The maintenance of active commercial relations with the Arab states and the states of Africa south of the Sahara which have signed agreements with us, and the concessions granted us with regard to certain raw materials, particularly a share of the Algerian oil, are not without value to us. Assuredly, what we derive from them is far less than what we give. But the very fact that a counterpart exists does not seem negligible to us, and it is obvious that we would be little inclined to furnish much to those who would furnish us nothing in return. Yet the importance of cooperation relates less to figures and immediate results than to the advantages of a general nature which it can ensure in the future for ourselves and our partners.

For the latter, in effect, the assistance given them, on condition that it is accompanied by an effort on their part, contributes little by little to advancing their material condition. But also by preparing—mentally, technically, practically—the people of these nations for the productive activities of our century, cooperation gradually puts them in a position to take their progress into their own hands. Thus, sooner or later, they will be able to furnish their own contribution to modern civilization. And, it is there that the world awaits them. For this is the question. If they succeed in taking their place in the development of humanity that our age is achieving, then their place will be assured in the society of states. But if they waste themselves in sterile agitations and contests, at home and abroad, then the world will soon see them as nothing more than areas of competition and possible battlefields for the great imperialist ambitions of today and tomorrow. As for France, it is evident that such a conclusion would lead her to take her aid and her hopes elsewhere. On the contrary, the success of peoples building in common with the people of France a work useful to all men, would not fail to extend her influence and her means of action. We see how high the goals are and how strong the reasons for cooperation.

But this is where the undertaking goes beyond the African context and actually constitutes a world-wide policy. By this means, France may turn toward other nations which, on other continents, are more or less broadly developing, which attract us by instinct and by nature and which, wishing for their development a support that will be given in our spirit and in our way, may desire to associate us directly with their progress and, reciprocally, take part in all that concerns France. . . .

No doubt the effort which we Frenchmen are capable of making materially in this regard is limited by our resources, which are not vast. But our own progress, which continues internally, affords us means which increase from year to year. Moreover, the problem for us often consists in bringing our friends the yeast of technical and cultural progress, which requires human capacities and cordial understanding even more than money. Lastly, we may believe that tomorrow's Europe, organized as we propose, would in solidarity with us play a larger part in this enterprise on which the fate of our species depends. Everything is related. What we are trying to do in order to create a Europe that will be itself falls in with what we are doing for the peoples rising within our civilization. Yes, cooperation is, henceforth, a great ambition of France.

ON NATIONAL INDEPENDENCE [5]

Question: Mr. President, France's diplomacy is based on the principle of national independence. The opponents of this principle say that it is outdated. Can this policy of national independence be reconciled with the aspirations of the peoples for greater unity in Europe?

Answer: We are in a century that has reached the two-thirds mark in its course, no more. However, since the turn of the century, the world has undergone changes unprecedented in their pace and their scope. Everything leads one to think that the trend is going to continue. For a whole series of facts of far-reaching significance is in the making to reshape the world.

In this series of facts, there is: the accession to sovereignty of a large number of states that have been created or restored since the war and, simultaneously, the unfolding of their reciprocal quarrels; the preponderant power acquired by two countries, America and Russia, which induces them to compete with each other and to align under their respective hegemonies the peoples within their reach; the extremely profound gestation that is taking place in enormous China and that destines her for a leading role in the world; the existence and increase in nuclear weapons capable of destroying great nations suddenly and utterly; finally and above all, the general driving force for progress that the opportunities of the modern industrial age are opening up in each region of the earth. In short, the world, in full evolution, is filled both with almost infinite hopes and gigantic dangers.

[5] From President de Gaulle's press conference, September 9, 1965. Text from *Atlantic Alliance: Allied Comment.* U.S. Congress. Senate. Committee on Government Operations. Supt. of Docs. Washington, D.C. 20402. '66. p 50-2.

Confronted with this situation, what can France's role be? But first, must France have a role? There is no lack of people, as you know, who think not. According to them, we—no longer being able to act by ourselves politically, economically, technically and militarily—should henceforth allow ourselves to be led by others. Moreover, the ideologies are there to cover up this renouncement. Thus some in our country, employing the screen of the International, would like to submit us to Moscow's obedience. Others, invoking either arbitrary theories or the convenience of interests, profess that our country should efface its personality in international organizations made in such a way that the United States can exercise in them, from within or without, a preponderant action with which, by definition, we have only to conform. It is in this way that those people conceive of our participation in the United Nations or NATO and desire that we see ourselves dissolved in a federation called "European" which would actually be "Atlantic."

Above all, it is a question of keeping ourselves free of any vassalage. It is true that, in many areas, we have the best reasons for associating with others. But on condition of retaining our self-determination. Thus, so long as the solidarity of the Western peoples appears to us necessary for the eventual defense of Europe, our country will remain the ally of her allies but, upon the expiration of the commitments formerly taken—that is, in 1969 by the latest—the subordination known as "integration" which is provided for by NATO and which hands our fate over to foreign authority shall cease, as far as we are concerned. Thus, while working to unite the states on both sides of the Rhine and the Alps, from the economic, political, cultural and strategic viewpoints, we are making sure that this organization does not deprive us of our free will. Thus, believing it right for an international system to regulate monetary relations, we do not recognize that the currency of any particular state has any automatic and privileged value in relation to gold, which is, which remains and which must remain, under the circumstances, the only real standard. Thus, having been, with four other powers, the founders of the United Nations, and desiring that it continue to be the meeting place of the delegations of all peoples and the open forum for their debates, we do not accept being bound, be it in the financial area, by armed interventions which contradict the Charter and to which we have not given our approval.

Moreover, it is by being this way that we believe we can, in the final analysis, best serve the alliance of free peoples, the European Community, the monetary institutions and the United Nations.

Indeed, the independence thus regained is enabling France to become, despite the ideologies and hegemonies of the colossi, for all the racial passions and prejudices, above and beyond the rivalries and ambitions of nations, a champion of cooperation, failing which the troubles, the interventions, the conflicts that lead to world war would go on spreading. Now, France is, par excellence, qualified to act in this way. She is so by her nature, which leads her to human contacts. She is so through the opinion that has historically been held of her and that opens to her a sort of latent credit when the universal is involved. She is so by the fact that she has freed herself of all the colonial holds she formerly exercised over other peoples. She is so, finally, because she appears to be a nation with free hands whose policy is not being determined by any pressure from without.

It is true that, in order to provide the means for living with dignity and for progress in turn to the two billion men who do not have them, an effort that goes far beyond the possibilities of France is required. Very fortunately, among the well-supplied countries, others besides us are also doing their share, although ours is the largest in proportion to our resources. But how much this aid, which is scattered and often opposed, would gain if it were combined on a large scale. In particular, what role could be played in this regard by a Europe that would want to unite. Specifically, the appeasement of our old torn continent, then the rapprochement of all the peoples that inhabit it, and finally their cooperation for their own development and the development of others—these constitute the essential goals—even if long-term ones—of French policy.

Thus with Germany, despite so many wounds suffered and grievances accumulated, we have concluded a treaty that—even if up to now it remains in a stage of cordial potentiality in many domains—however provides for periodic meetings between the two governments and is bearing fruit in such areas as culture and youth contacts. Thus with five of our neighbors we have formed the beginnings of an economic community, which we want to hope it will one day be possible to complete, and we have proposed to them organizing at least political cooperation.

Thus our contacts and our exchanges are multiplying with the countries of the East, each of them, of course, being treated only in consideration of its national personality. In this respect, we attach great importance to the new trend of our relations with Russia. We are pleased with the results achieved on the occasion of [Rumanian] President Maurer's visit with respect to French-Rumanian relations. With great pleasure we are going to receive [Polish] President Cyrankiewicz, hoping that his presence here will serve the practical rapprochement of the French and Polish peoples, friends and allies at all times in their history. We do not hesitate to envisage that the day will come when, in order to achieve a constructive entente from the Atlantic to the Urals, all of Europe will wish to settle its own problems and, above all, that of Germany, by the only means that will make it possible to do so—that of a general agreement. On that day, our continent could once again assume in the world, for the good of all men, the role that is worthy of its resources and its capacities.

ON FRENCH AND RUSSIAN COOPERATION [6]

Russia and France go back rather far into the past; they have both experienced sufficient trials, the most serious of which were the most recent. They discern quite clearly the dangers and the hopes that the world of the present holds, to weigh well the importance of today's meeting.

[6] From "French and Russian Cooperation, a European Problem," address by Charles de Gaulle delivered in Moscow, June 23, 1966. Text from *Vital Speeches of the Day*. 32:589-90. Jl. 15, '66. Reprinted by permission.

We French pay you a visit, convinced that there is reason to strengthen and multiply, in all fields, the relations between our two countries. We think, in fact, that more direct and broader cooperation by them should help Europe set forth on the path of union and the world on that of balance, progress and peace.

And is this not what is above all at issue? To be sure, under the really quite different regimes established in their countries by the highly diverse vicissitudes of their national and international existence, all modern nations in this industrial age are similarly pursuing the goals and are bowing to the laws of the same mechanical and scientific civilization and, as a result, actually have more reasons than ever before for understanding one another and for collaborating. But other conditions run counter to these prospects. The world war, as it was launched and conducted by the ambition we know, has produced in the world, and first in Europe, a dislocation and rendings that have not yet mended.

On the other hand, the sudden rise in the relative power of two great states—America and the Soviet Union—as well as the opposition of their respective ideologies, have led them to compete, while around them their neighbors were split into two blocs and the cold war spread over the world. Lastly, the nuclear armaments built on both sides, although their frightening potential makes their owners cautious, nevertheless maintains between them an atmosphere of fear and distrust that keeps them from drawing closer together.

That is why France, for her part, is not satisfied with this rigid confrontation of the two organizations. Without ceasing, quite the contrary, to be a country of freedom and a Western nation par excellence, she would like to see the harmful spell broken and, at least insofar as she is concerned, the start of the implementation of new relations with the so-called Eastern European states, toward détente, entente and cooperation.

To be sure, it is first with the Soviet Union that she hopes to achieve this. The reasons for this primary choice are obvious. Russia is, indeed and in all respects, the leading power in the part of the world where she is located. Secondly, she seems to

France to be an interlocutor with whom understanding and collaboration are natural to the highest degree.

This is a political and actual reality as old as our two countries, which is based on their history and geography, on the fact that no basic grievance has ever made them opposed . . . and finally on affinities that are clearly expressed, both on the level of their intellectual, literary, artistic and scientific elites and between their peoples. It goes without saying that their alliances during the world wars, and in particular the vital role that the Soviet Union played in the decisive victory that ended the second, only strengthened among the French the feeling of this solidarity. In short, since the international situation needs to be guided in the right direction, to speak about this to the East, Paris necessarily addresses itself to Moscow.

All the more so since for France, without her disregarding in any way the essential role that the United States has to play in the pacification and transformation of the world, it is the restoration of Europe as a productive whole, instead of its being paralyzed by a sterile division, that is the primary condition. Also, an entente between hitherto antagonistic states is above all, to the French, a European problem. This holds true for intellectual and material exchanges that promote common progress. This holds true for the settlement that will one day have to determine the destiny of all Germany and the security of our continent. This holds true for what must be done so that Asia, Latin America and Africa are also guaranteed peace and, moreover, helped in the efforts that they are exerting for their own development.

Until the time when all of Europe reaches the point of finding together the ways and means that would lead it to these essential goals, everything, in our view, commits France and the Soviet Union to do so between themselves right now.

ON VIETNAM, NATO, AND GERMANY [7]

We are certain there can be no military victory enabling the Americans to subdue the Vietnamese. And neither do we believe

[7] From "Excerpts from President de Gaulle's Remarks at His News Conference," October 28, 1966. Text from the New York *Times.* p 8. O. 29, '66.

in the possibility that the Vietnamese can destroy the United States forces.

So we are proposing no mediation whatsoever, which nobody would accept and which would lead nowhere. Nonetheless, we find it totally detestable that a small country should be bombed by a very big one, and we find not less detestable that the soldiers of both sides should suffer losses.

But we are not offering any peace plan for the good reason that, at the moment, peace is impossible. This does not prevent us from indicating as clearly as possible what are, in our opinion, the conditions that could lead one day to negotiations to end the war.

These conditions depend indeed on the decision of the Americans. For them it would be a matter of observing the principle according to which each people should settle its affairs in its own way and by itself. The Americans would have to apply this principle to the Vietnamese people.

Consequently, they would have to bring back to America the forces that, little by little, they have sent to Vietnam after the departure of our forces. They would also have to accept as the basis of a future settlement a real and effectively controlled neutrality of Southeast Asia and assistance needed to help it patch up its ruins and resume its development.

Finally, the Americans would have to recognize that in Asia no agreement, no important treaty, is valid without the participation of China, and they would have to draw the conclusions as regards relations to be established with this great state and as regards its rightful place in the United Nations.

It is true that American policy and opinion at the moment are not—it is the least one can say—going in this direction and that, consequently, the position taken by France in this respect offends many people on the other side of the Atlantic. We are convinced that there is no other conceivable solution.

If we talk about it so outspokenly, it is because we gave an example not so long ago in Algeria by taking on ourselves—and believe me, it was meritorious—to give way to peace there.

We are doing so also because we are, among the Western nations, the one that, no doubt, is most attached to the peoples of Indochina.

And finally we are doing so because of our friendship for America, a friendship that, since the beginning, led us unceasingly to try to dissuade her from this fateful undertaking.

NATO

The fact that France should recover her independence in the defense field was thought by many to be impossible. Some even said it was ridiculous or dangerous for our security or of a nature to jeopardize our international situation. France is doing it nonetheless.

So far one cannot see what kind of disaster this can lead to. As of now, although the Atlantic alliance remains the same as when we created it in 1949, there is for us no subordination, neither at present nor in the future, of our forces to a foreign authority.

Case-by-Case Basis

In five months [roughly, by April 1, 1967—Ed.], no staff headquarters, no unit, no base of any allied army will remain on our territory. Military personnel and equipment, warships and aircraft wishing to pass through our territory will do so by an authorization we will give them on a case-to-case basis.

This is the core of the matter: an international situation, in which two superstates would alone have arms capable of annihilating any other country, would alone have the means through dissuasion of insuring their own security, would alone maintain each its own camp of committed peoples under their command. Such a situation, in the long run, could only paralyze and sterilize the rest of the universe, which would be submitted either to a crushing competition or to the yoke of a double hegemony that would be agreed upon by the two rivals.

In such conditions how could Europe unite, how could Latin America assert itself, how could Africa follow its own path, how could China find its place and how could the United Nations become a really efficient organization?

"Who Could Regret It?"

Since America and the Soviet Union are not destroying their ultimate weapons, we had to break the spell. And we have broken it, we are breaking it as far as we are concerned, and through our own means.

As France is breaking this stifling rigidity, we shall see and we already see diminishing the constant and seriously dangerous game called the cold war. And who could regret it?

The concept we have of Europe and the actions we carry out there are naturally ours, but they are directed against nobody, and we even think that they can be useful to everybody. It is true that their foundation is Europe, such as it is and not such as one could imagine it was, and as it is not.

It is also true that what we are trying to do there aims at serving its interests, and not interests outside it. We believe that our continent must, by itself, from one end of its territory to the other, organize relaxation of tension, understanding and then cooperation.

Such is the inspiration of our European policy, whether in our relations with Germany, our enemy of yesterday, or in our efforts for the organization of an economic and—perhaps one day —political grouping of the Six, or in what we are doing to agree and to associate ourselves with the Eastern countries.

Germany

As for Germany, despite the terrible losses inflicted on us by wars begun and unleashed by the First Reich and then by the Third Reich, we have offered her a frank reconciliation. We concluded, at her request, a treaty that could have served as a basis for cooperation in the fields of politics, economy, culture and defense. It is not our doing if the preferential contacts ceaselessly developed by Bonn with Washington have deprived this French-German agreement of inspiration and substance.

However, we have gone back neither on forgetting our grievances nor on the practice of cordial relations with Federal Germany. And while preserving, there as elsewhere, the entire control of our forces, we consent for the moment to maintain on its territory a large military force, which, of course, serves its security, and which we will withdraw the moment it asks us to, and for which, unlike its other allies, we ask no financial compensation.

On the other hand, the European Economic Community, the Common Market of the Six, if it has been possible to organize, it has been with the very active participation of France. I wish to stress that on many occasions it is the determination and firmness of the action of French authorities that has prevented the enterprise from losing itself in roads that had no exit.

III. THE DE GAULLE DIPLOMACY

EDITOR'S INTRODUCTION

There was a time, not so long ago, when France was a power in Africa and Asia. Those days are gone forever, but the French presence remains strong in many areas of the globe. One of the reasons for this is that the French language and French culture are an important part of life in many of these former colonial territories. Another reason is that de Gaulle has made a determined effort to offer the developing countries an alternative to either the United States or the U.S.S.R.—and some of the low-income nations have responded favorably to this chance. De Gaulle has argued the case for France through the liberal use of foreign aid in Africa, through the continued export of French culture around the world, through frequent travel and through a succession of imaginative diplomatic moves.

This section of the volume singles out several aspects of French policy toward the developing countries. The first article discusses at length the former French African colonies, which de Gaulle had hoped to mold into a viable community of independent states looking to France for leadership. The author makes the point that although the Community, for all practical purposes, does not exist, the bonds between France and its former colonies are nevertheless strong. The next article, from the *Wall Street Journal,* discusses de Gaulle's efforts to win new influence for France in Southeast Asia. The following piece analyzes French diplomatic and economic policy toward China. The author, J. S. Prybyla, weighs the possible advantages as well as the problems of such relations. The final article in this section offers a retrospective look at French involvement in Vietnam after World War II (when Vietnam was still part of Indochina) and speaks of current French efforts to achieve a settlement in that part of the world.

THE FRENCH COMMUNITY—DOES IT EXIST? [1]

The original Franco-African Communauté [Community] established in 1958 by Title XII of the constitution of the Fifth French Republic is dead, and its institutional successors are weak. Nonetheless, an informal political relationship and close economic and cultural ties exist between France and most French-speaking independent states of Africa, and a larger, non-institutionalized, cultural group—embracing all countries in the world where French is an official or important language—is not without importance in world affairs.

In the twenty years since the end of World War II, there has been a series of complex organizations and institutions linking France and Africa. One reason for the complexity and subsequent lack of clarity about the nature of Franco-African relations was the attempt on the part of the French governments of the Fourth Republic and the early Fifth Republic to avoid giving independence to the colonies.

Many Frenchmen feared that without colonies France would lose its power, that it would become a country of 45 million people instead of a Grand Ensemble of over 100 million. Although any thought of independence was resisted (at the same time that the British were beginning to set tentative dates for the independence of their colonies), it was necessary for the French to come to terms with the pressures for change—the result of promises made during World War II, the war in Indochina and then in Algeria, the demands of the Afro-Asian Bandung Conference of 1955, the independence of Morocco and Tunisia, the independence of Ghana, and the increasing danger of civil strife in France itself.

The changes France offered the colonies of black Africa amounted to freedom without independence. Africans were increasingly free to be Frenchmen in a Grand Ensemble without being given the independence to be Africans. The French Empire had become the French Union during the Fourth Republic, and many Africans became French citizens. African representatives to

[1] From article by Brian Weinstein, faculty member in the African Studies & Research Program of Howard University, Washington, D.C. *Current History*. 50:214-20+. Ap. '66. Reprinted by permission.

French legislative bodies helped make French laws, and local assemblies permitted some participation in colonial affairs. Changes . . . [in] June 1956 gave the peoples of the colonies much more voice in their own destiny. In 1958, the French Union was transformed into the Communauté with the return to power of General Charles de Gaulle as president and the establishment of the Fifth Republic.

According to the proposed constitution of the Fifth Republic, the member states of a Franco-African Community were to have "autonomy" with the power to "administer themselves and manage their own affairs" (Article 77); but control over foreign affairs, finances, and mineral resources would be the responsibility of the Community as a whole (Article 78). The institutions of the Community were organized so that France would maintain its control over it. The president was the president of France assisted by an executive council representative of all members but without more than an advisory role. A senate and a court of arbitration had a majority of French representatives.

The 1958 Referendum

Black African adults and metropolitan Frenchmen were given the choice in the referendum of September 1958 of accepting or rejecting the new constitution and the Community which it was supposed to establish. Rejection would mean independence, or "secession," as some Frenchmen called it. Article 86 indicated simply that a member of the Community could become independent but that it would then cease to belong to the organization. During his tour of Africa to build support for a "yes" vote, General de Gaulle emphasized that any country could choose independence by a negative vote but that independence would bring certain "consequences"—a cessation of aid programs, for example. Independence would, therefore, be punished.

When Guinea voted no, declared its independence, and requested association with that Community which all other territories had approved, the French government withdrew aid and personnel. A year after Ghana had become independent and had joined the British Commonwealth, France still rejected the idea of independence as an acceptable choice for one of its colonies.

Regardless of the French position, independence was inevitable, and when Mali decided it would declare its independence in 1960, an attempt to save the Community was made by altering the constitution. A law tacked on to the constitution recognized independence and association as compatible:

A member state of the Community may, also, by way of agreements, become independent without thereby ceasing to belong to the Community. [Constitutional Law, 4 June, 1960.]

This final recognition of independence as a legitimate choice for Africans came too late. Ivory Coast declared its independence before making any "agreements" with France as stipulated, and in the course of 1960 all former members became independent. French refusal to recognize independence before 1960 had destroyed the possibility of an institutionalized grouping of French and African states.

The Communauté was never officially dissolved, although its institutions no longer function. Some Frenchmen and Africans have chosen to believe it still exists. Attached to the office of the French president is, for example, a secretariat for the Community and African-Malagasy affairs. Troops under French command sent to Gabon in February 1964, to crush a coup d'état were called "the Army of the Community" by the Gabonese chief-of-state. Most French newspapers referred to them simply as French troops (which they were).

France has not formally been a member of organizations which have succeeded the Community, but it is clear that French support is important for their survival. . . .

All these organizations have been criticized since 1960 as barriers to African unity and as neocolonialist enterprises by means of which France is reputed to continue to control the destinies of former colonies. More important than these organizations in maintaining French influence are the frequent informal meetings in Paris between African presidents and President de Gaulle, meetings with the French minister of cooperation, the presence of French technical advisers in many African ministries,

French control over the Franc Zone (to which most countries belong), and the importance of France as a trading partner. French administrators, advisers and troops are returning to France, although a contingent still protects the president of Gabon and highly mobile units will be stationed at three African bases.

Problems of Development

In twenty-one of the thirty-six independent countries of Africa [since this article was written additional African countries have gained their independence—Ed.] French is at least one of the official languages. The total population of these francophonic [French-speaking] countries is between 90 and 100 million. Belgium ruled in three—Congo (Leopoldville), Rwanda and Burundi. Algeria was a part of France; the French ministry of foreign affairs had charge of the protectorates of Morocco and Tunisia, and the "rue Oudinot" (the ministry for overseas France) governed the fifteen colonies of black Africa and Madagascar.

These fifteen which, with the exception of Guinea, voted for the Community, have a total population of about 45 million, or 10 million less than one former British colony, Nigeria. Underpopulation, the absence of a national tradition, and their close ties with France differentiate these countries from the rest of Africa. Their most important problems are unity and legitimacy, identity and self-confidence, and meaningful change. . . .

The failure of some governments to solve real problems and of one or two leaders to recognize their duties to the nation, plus destructive corruption, have weakened Africans' faith in the promises of independence and have encouraged the military to seize power. Absence of meaningful change encourages cynicism and the withdrawal of intellectuals from political involvement; it also gives further strength to those who believe in the Chinese type of Communist revolution. Attempts to bring about meaningful change and progress have been sincerely undertaken in most countries, but the problems are far more complex than anyone realized. These problems must ultimately be solved by Africans, but the programs of assistance from France are playing an important role.

French Assistance

Nowhere does there seem to have been a greater effort to convince the average person of the necessity of aid programs for Africa than in France. French programs have been comparatively large. France has contributed more than 1 per cent of its gross national product to African assistance while the United States has contributed less than 1 per cent in nonmilitary assistance. (In terms of total dollars spent each year the United States has had a much larger program, of course.) The total French bilateral aid to black Africa has decreased from almost $1 billion in 1961 to less than $500 million, but some multilateral programs have increased, and the type of aid is changing.

The government has tried to convince all citizens of the need for a large aid effort. Polls have been taken to prove that most Frenchmen really favor assistance to Africa, particularly to former French colonies. The president emphasizes the need for such programs in his public addresses, and fairly objective studies show the effects of aid. The 1963 Clay Report on American foreign aid was a mere 25 pages long. The two-volume Jeanneney Report submitted to the French government in the same year was 100 pages long with almost 300 pages of specialized studies of the needs of developing nations and the role of France. The French Economic and Social Council, an advisory body, has undertaken numerous studies of specific French aid efforts and the general assistance program. Its most recent study showed how complex the organization of French assistance is.

Ministries which had colonial responsibilities have taken over aid programs. A new ministry of cooperation is in charge of assistance to those countries once under the ministry for Overseas France and controls certain agencies which used to be attached to the "rue Oudinot." The ministry of foreign affairs holds responsibility for projects in Morocco, Tunisia and Guinea. It also supervises bilateral programs with all other countries. It sends teachers and technicians, grants scholarships, and manages cultural centers. Activities of the ministry of foreign affairs come into conflict with other ministries such as the ministry of cooperation in former

Belgian territories like Congo (Leopoldville) where French influence is increasing. A special secretariat attached to the office of the premier supervises relations with Algeria, still considered as different from all other African states.

The ministry of finances plays a key role through its Caisse Centrale de Coopération Économique. The Caisse could coordinate all aid efforts because it disburses money for other ministries such as the ministry of cooperation. It can also lend money on its own for purposes of investment and has been in charge of disbursement of the important subsidies granted to maintain a high price for African crops like coffee and cotton. The Common Market has undertaken to subsidize these crops. Other ministries—like the ministry of education which controls universities in Senegal, Ivory Coast, Dahomey, Cameroon, Congo (Brazzaville) and Madagascar —have very specific and more limited functions.

"Cooperation"

The government prefers to aid former colonies in Africa instead of aiding other countries and increasingly emphasizes education. The terms used to explain this double emphasis are "cooperation" and "defense." The word "cooperation" refers to all those relations and projects between France and materially underdeveloped nations which contribute to the further development of the latter. The emphasis, the French say, is on mutual respect and mutual aid. Cooperation and the ministry of cooperation are, the French insist, above every-day politics and the vicissitudes of international relations. According to the Jeanneney Report, a key justification for it is a sense of human solidarity. "Cooperation" most often describes relations between France and the former members of the Community, while "technical assistance" and other terms describe aid programs to other countries.

It is necessary, French leaders say, to make an *effort particulier* [special effort] in the francophonic countries of black Africa and Madagascar because of their historical ties with France, the friendship which prevails, the absence of language problems and the relative proximity of the countries. The money for this *effort particulier* comes from the Fonds d'Aide et de Coopération (FAC) of the ministry of cooperation. It supports research, teachers, French technicians and administrators, scholarships, training programs in France and in Africa, economic planning projects, and the activities of several public and semi-public agencies. FAC used to subsidize the annual budgets of most members of the Community, but its role in this area has been substantially reduced. It has also decreased the total number of French administrators or *conseillers techniques* [technical advisers] who, in the first years of independence, were more important than the African ministers themselves.

Decreases in personnel and in money spent by the ministry of cooperation indicate a change in the orientation of cooperation. In spite of the fact that the total French personnel in Africa has decreased, the number of teachers, and scholarship and training programs have increased. Teachers in Africa under the ministry of cooperation have doubled since 1960 and, counting the contributions of all ministries, there are almost 10,000 French teachers in the fourteen states of the old Community. Another 10,000 teachers are in Algeria, and about 14,000 have been sent by the ministry of foreign affairs all over the world.

All fourteen members of the former Community signed the Yaoundé Convention of July 1963, and thereby agreed to continue an association with the Common Market which had begun five years earlier, before independence. (Four other African states —Congo [Leopoldville], Rwanda, Burundi, and Somalia—also signed.) A free trade area between the six European countries and Africa insures a market for African products (as well as European products), and between 1963 and 1968 the Common Market's European Development Fund is supposed to spend $800 million to aid these eighteen associated states. France has pledged almost one third of this fund and has considerable influence over the ways the money is used in these former colonial outposts in Africa.

Bilateral Programs

In spite of France's participation in a multilateral program of assistance through the Common Market, it has had strong preferences for bilateral programs. Only about one fortieth of all aid to underdeveloped countries goes through international oganizations, compared with about one seventeenth for the United States. The French premier has explained why this is so: "The fundamental reason for keeping a bilateral aid program is our effort with regard to the French language."

The French government believes that an indicator of French power is the number of countries where French is an important language and where French culture is highly esteemed. Bilateral programs and the Common Market, in which the French voice is loud and clear, can best promote the language and defend it where it is already spoken. French-speaking people will, the government believes, understand and support French policies; they will purchase French products; and they will be living testimony to the quality of Gallic culture which must be defended in those countries where old ties with France are threatened by the Soviet Union, China, and the "Anglo-Saxons." To preserve the predominance of French the government, therefore, emphasizes aid to education. It also wishes to expand its influence into the anglophonic countries and into Latin America, but present programs are modest.

The United States has lately respected French desires for hegemony in the former Community, and American aid programs have actually decreased since 1962. . . . France remains suspicious of the United States, however, because of what is believed to have been the American role in the diminution of French influence in the Far East, North Africa and the Middle East.

A New Community?

Close links between France and the former Communauté continue; clear French hegemony in these countries is a source of power for France and a source of aid for the Africans. In international organizations most of these countries add their votes to that of France, and French opinion has more weight. Uranium from Gabon helps build the French nuclear force, and other minerals like manganese, iron and aluminum, plus wood products, earn foreign exchange for the Franc Zone and satisfy some French needs.

Because of the expense to France, not all Frenchmen favor assistance. At the same time, many Africans desire more freedom to solve their problems utilizing the experience of countries other than France. Because the United States, when it limits aid programs, discourages this exercise in freedom, French-speaking Africans increasingly turn to the Soviet Union and China.

French language, culture and a certain shared history will continue to link France with these black African countries. Admiration for France remains important even in those countries whose political relations with the former colonial power are poor. Guinea, for example, has continued to send students in law and the arts and sciences to Paris, while technicians are sent to the Soviet Union and the United States for training. In Senegal, where relations are good, President Léopold Senghor has said that even though the University of Dakar will become independent of French government control, it will remain a French language university in the French tradition because of the superiority of this language.

Another type of community exists between France and other countries, many of which have a French cultural tradition. The image of France under the leadership of General de Gaulle as a country independent of the United States attracts the support and admiration of the developing nations and of several European nations. The end of the war in Algeria, recognition of Communist China, development of an independent nuclear force, criticisms of American policies in Vietnam and even in Latin America have contributed to the image of France as a leader in world affairs.

Even though an independent France, caught like other nations between the superpowers, has only moderate power, France has served as an example to others and has permitted them more flexibility in international affairs by association with it. Several countries or areas are renewing old links with France. By increasing its ties with France as part of a *révolution tranquille* [peaceful revolution], Quebec province, for example, is able to assert its autonomy in Canada: "In our own way, we are the representatives of French culture in North America, and we intend to fulfill the responsibilities which result from this situation," the prime minister of Quebec has written.

Agreements between East European countries like Rumania and Bulgaria, where French is still spoken, permit these countries to assert some independence from the Soviet Union. The same attitude influences some Latin American leaders with regard to the United States. Ties with Lebanon and Iran may be strengthened. Saint Joseph's University in Beirut is a French university and is a French cultural center in the Middle East. In both Cambodia and Laos, French is used extensively in schools, and leaders of these countries have looked to France for leadership. Although France has little political influence in Vietnam at present, its cultural influence is strong and France may well play a future role.

President Habib Bourguiba of Tunisia said on a recent trip to other African countries that a francophonic commonwealth should be organized. Because of the great diversity of the countries where French is an important language or where there is support for independent French policies, it is unlikely that such a commonwealth would be as important to France as the present ties with the former African colonies. It is also unlikely that members of such a commonwealth would be willing to follow French leadership as closely as the former members of the Community.

Nonetheless, with comparatively few resources France has made use of the concept of community at two levels to further its own national interest. Both exist above considerations of race, religion, national identity and ideology. In the process of reasserting its own importance in international affairs, partly through these communities, France has made a contribution to the weakening of a rigid and dangerous polarization of the world.

IN ASIA: A DRIVE FOR INFLUENCE [2]

One hundred and two years ago a French officer leveled a pistol at the ruler of Cambodia and forced him to turn his country into a French protectorate.

Today, that ruler's great-grandson, chief of state Prince Norodom Sihanouk, welcomes another French officer to Cambodia under far more friendly circumstances. Despite ninety years of French domination, which ended in 1954, Cambodia under Prince Sihanouk is going all out to give French President Charles de Gaulle a lavish reception during his three-day visit. . . .

President de Gaulle is to speak before 100,000 Cambodians at the huge Complexe Sportif, an athletic center. He'll dine in the ruins of Angkor Wat, twelfth century Asia's most impressive architectural relic. To avoid any chance of an ugly incident, Cambodian officials have warned citizens to stay away from open windows and balconies; even gasoline tanks at service stations along the president's route are being emptied to reduce the possibility of an explosion. Antiaircraft batteries have been positioned should "unfriendly" planes appear.

France: A "True Friend"

The reception for "le grand Charles" points up the enormous prestige that France still commands . . . in Asia, notwithstanding its long history of heavy-handed colonial rule. France, says Prince Sihanouk, a vociferous critic of Western imperialism, is one of Cambodia's "very rare true friends." And President de Gaulle's visit, far from being an isolated example of French interest in Southeast Asia, is just one dramatic step in a calculated campaign, now two years old, to reassert French influence here.

The French effort, at times is annoying United States policymakers if not directly clashing with them. A major aim of Gaullist policy is to undermine American influence in the area by taking the lead in ending the war in Vietnam. "The longer the war continues, the more French influence is eroded," a European

[2] From "France & Far East: De Gaulle Spurs Effort to Win New Influence in Old Asian Colonies," by Robert Keatley, staff reporter. *Wall Street Journal.* p 1+. Ag. 30, '66. Reprinted by permission.

diplomatic observer notes. "Thus, if France wants to strengthen its ties in Indochina (the old name given colonial Laos, Cambodia, and Vietnam), it must remove this region from struggle by neutralizing it." . . .

Peacemaker de Gaulle?

It's not that France could somehow quickly restore peace where the best efforts of others have failed. The war is expected to be fought or ended by those nations with military strength in Southeast Asia, and France has none. But President de Gaulle would leap at the chance to act as mediator between the belligerents in Vietnam and thus possibly fall heir to the laurels of the successful peacemaker, political analysts say. Such a coup would enhance his goal of restoring France to the status of a true world power and becoming the leader of a "third force" of nations committed neither to East nor West.

There are less altruistic reasons, too, behind the current French effort. Though President de Gaulle is motivated by lofty ideals, some other French leaders are said to be piqued by the growing United States role in Southeast Asia and would be most disturbed should the United States succeed in the kind of war at which the French failed miserably twelve years ago. Also, some former *colons,* or French colonial residents, would like to expand their economic interests in the area that was once Indochina, though diplomats agree that President de Gaulle himself cares little about the economic aspects.

In fact, French recognition of the Communist government in China two years ago hasn't become the financial bonanza that was expected. Total French sales to China last year reached only $60 million, just $1 million more than in 1963, the year before relations were resumed. There's confident talk of greater trade ahead, though, and last December the French staged the biggest trade fair ever sponsored in Peking by Westerners; 345 French companies exhibited $10 million worth of goods. Air France soon will become the first Western line to fly scheduled flights to mainland China.

Pompidou and Venus de Milo

The French effort in Asia extends beyond China and Indochina. President de Gaulle recently dispatched two noted Parisians—Premier Georges Pompidou and Venus de Milo—to Japan to promote France there. A new French trade center opened three months ago in downtown Tokyo, complete with aperitifs and quotations from the Paris Bourse, or stock exchange, next door to an American trade center. Later this year, President de Gaulle is expected to meet with Japan's foreign minister to discuss stronger trade ties between the two industrial (and protectionist) nations.

Meanwhile, a new French ambassador, experienced in the petroleum industry, has been sent to oil-rich Indonesia, where France still supplies a little foreign aid. The French have discussed the possibility of greater aid to Asian nations, while steadfastly refusing to take part in the United States backed Asian Development Bank.

It's here in former Indochina, though, that the French hand remains strongest. The French presence is sometimes casually deceptive. France's embassy in Saigon, for example, has been padlocked since a diplomatic rift last year, but consular officials regularly use the back door, and they occupy offices in the building.

French cultural influence is pervasive and expanding. Concerts and art shows are part of the picture, but the French also are trying the wholesale export of French methods and attitudes to turn local recipients into ardent Francophiles. Politically motivated, the French program is aimed at the elite of Southeast Asia; the French wish to turn the most influential Asians to Paris, rather than London, New York or Peking, when they need guidance in any matter.

Each year France spends $3 million in South Vietnam and $2 million in Laos on education. Altogether, about 1,000 French teachers in Cambodia, Laos and Vietnam are paid by the French government. It bankrolls eight primary schools and five *lycées,* or high schools, that teach 12,000 upper-class children in the French language. Another 20,000 children study in private French schools, mostly Catholic, where courses also are taught in French and oriented markedly toward things Parisian. [Many of the French schools in Vietnam were recently closed by order of the government—Ed.]

These institutions are by far superior to others in the lands of old Indochina. A Vietnam cabinet minister who frets over the political implications of French schooling concedes that he sends his own children to the French schools because others have such low standards.

The French mission in Laos blocked an American attempt to help expand and modernize the school system. After twelve years of considerable assistance by the United States, Vietnam's university faculties are still dominated by Francophiles. "The United States has just made no impact," says an American educational adviser.

Professors trained in the United States find themselves passed over when promotions and salary increases are handed out; the French-leaning university administrators call American education "technical" and therefore inferior. French-trained medical professors for two years stalled an American effort to build a new medical school in Saigon, according to a former Vietnam cabinet minister. The rector of Vietnam's largest university still clings to his French citizenship.

In Cambodia schools are also controlled by French or French-trained administrators. A French *lycée* in North Vietnam managed to carry on without being closed until last year. In the capital of Communist China itself, there are sixty instructors from France, far more than China has permitted from any other Western nation.

Diplomatic observers argue that the French cultural effort is far more subtle and sophisticated than that of the United States. In Saigon's Vietnamese-American Association school, for example, critics complain that too much time is spent teaching bar girls and shop assistants how to talk with GI's. The French, by contrast, are said to view their language as a tool for shaping ideas and attitudes, including political ones.

The French library in Saigon stacks 50,000 volumes in an air-conditioned building. The library is considered superior to its American counterpart run by the United States Information Service. Many of the one hundred French magazines in the library feature political articles denouncing United States policy in Asia.

Militarily and economically, the French also are trying to increase their influence in Southeast Asia. Paris gave Laos $3 million in aid when King Savang Vatthana dropped in to visit President de Gaulle this summer; in recent years, French aid to the country has run as high as $7 million. In Cambodia, France maintains a 400-man military training mission; when a United States Army group was there it was restricted to supply functions.

Frenchmen still own 80 per cent of South Vietnam's rubber plantations, carry on much of the country's banking activities, and bottle Saigon's 33 and LaRue brand beers—besides Coca Cola. A French company owns 35 per cent of a Cambodia venture that will build the country's first oil refinery, and Prince Sihanouk has made it clear he doesn't intend to nationalize French interests. Though nobody trades much with Laos, a French company there hopes soon to start exporting tin.

The French influence often has maintained itself despite French policy rather than because of it. Unhappy experiences under French colonialism shaped the anti-Western attitudes of generations of educated Indochinese. Nationalist politicians were hounded by French police, jailed, exiled, and driven underground, creating a heritage that still survives in conspiratorial Vietnamese politicking.

The considerable volume of francs that Frenchmen poured into Southeast Asia under colonial rule were aimed almost wholly at benefiting French investors. The economic invasion disrupted traditional patterns of land tenure, impoverished many rural folk, and corrupted the once-superb Indochinese handicrafts industry. Under French rule, also, all important colonial government jobs in Indochina went to French citizens.

PARIS-PEKING TRADE [3]

France's diplomatic and economic courting of Communist China is based on a typically de Gaullian long-range analysis of the international scene in which sober realism and grandiose delusion are about equally mixed. The realism is largely economic: France needs new export markets for its growing industries, and Communist China by virtue of its determination, if nothing else, looks very much like the right recipe for France's export hunger. Moreover, the Anglo-Saxons across the Channel are doing their level best to convince Peking to buy in England the very things France is eager to sell.

Trade with China—this promising market of 700 million people short on foreign exchange but long on ambition—is therefore, for the French a matter of domestic importance and urgency. De Gaulle's lingering suspicion that the Anglo-Saxons speak with one voice (usually American), while they wheel and deal as best they can (often at French expense), makes American ideological pontifications sound hollow in French official ears. At this point the transition from realism to *mystique* is almost complete. France's need is the civilized world's interest, for each man has two countries: his own and France. The unconvinced regard France's hypothetical future influence in Southeast Asia with considerable misgivings, trade or no trade. They point out that most of the militant leaders of North Vietnam and China (and, they add, of Albania as well) are the products of France's seats of higher learning. It is no consolation that the Albanians read the *Peking Review* in its elegant French edition. If Chinese silks were exchanged for French *lycées* rather than for French fertilizer, and if the new generation of Chinese were to drink at the source of French culture not only avidly but deeply—which, it would seem, their fathers had never done—things might be different. As it is, argue the irreverent, it is better to call matters by their name: a healthy respect for the franc . . . is not foreign to French character, nor is it necessary to dress up in pompous

[3] From "Paris-Peking Trade: Marianne & the Dragon," by Jan S. Prybyla, associate professor of economics at Pennsylvania State University. *Nation.* 200:99-102. F. 1, '65. Reprinted by permission.

phrases about culture and the intellect what is, after all, a perfectly normal preoccupation with money.

Like the cynics of Anglo-Saxon extraction, the Russians have their moments of ulcerous soul searching. . . . In blunt terms, the Soviets tax the Chinese with sounding off like Confucius and behaving like Trotsky. When the Russians strike a bargain or two with the West, they are accused by the self-righteous Chinese Puritans of selling out to the imperialists; when the Chinese do more of the same, it suddenly becomes a question of dealing creatively with the "intermediate zone," a makeshift concept of doubtful Marxist lineage, but useful to cover up the Chinese need for wheat, machines and fertilizer which the Soviets have since 1960 refused to fill. An "intermediate zoner" in Chinese, is a capitalist imperialist who sells sulphur-resistant pipe to Peking.

The French qualify. A Chinese petrochemical mission which visited Paris in the early spring of 1964, combined side trips to the Louvre with a thorough inspection of French natural-gas processing equipment. Since the development of the Saharan oil fields and the natural-gas deposits of the Lacq region in south-western France, the French have made impressive strides in chemical engineering. In fact, potential output of equipment has far outstripped demand, thus turning a technical achievement into a nagging economic headache. It happens that China's natural gas has a high sulphur content. The French have a transmission pipe that withstands sulphur-induced wear and tear. They can also offer equipment for oil refineries, automation installations, measuring, control and mining equipment, complete factories, plants for the production of natural gas, rolling mills for thin steel sheet, stainless tubes and sheet, and many other components of industrialization.

To acquaint Chinese buyers with French technical achievements, an exhibition of precision instruments was opened in Peking in September 1964 under the sponsorship of a theoretically private but in fact semi-official body. This exhibition, the first such French-sponsored event to be held in China since the end of the war, will be followed in November 1965 by a much more ambitious industrial fair in which all of France's major industries are expected to take part. For the Chinese, exhibitions of this kind are one means of securing technical information, an objective high on China's scale of priorities. The French instrumentation exhibit was visited in the course of three weeks by more than 60,000 Chinese engineers, technicians, university professors and students. The Chinese made only one complaint: the French had not displayed the latest technical achievements. On January 11, 1964, the French enterprises, "Speichim" and S.A. Melle, concluded a contract with the China National Technical Import Corporation for the delivery of complete equipment for an N-butyl and ethylhexyl alcohol plant worth about $5 million.

France's emphasis on exports of capital equipment is understandable, not only because of the capacity ailments of the French producers' goods sector but also in view of the unbalanced pattern of French exports to China so far. France has joined Canada, Australia and Argentina in the great wheat rush to China which followed on Mao's commune debacle and Khrushchev's "I told you so" refusal to extend a helping Socialist hand. The Russians were hampered by their own virgin land problems and a tight foreign-exchange situation, yet while the grain may not have been there, neither was the necessary fraternal spirit. It was then that the "intermediate zone" came in handy: in 1961, 1962 and again in 1963, French exports to China consisted overwhelmingly of cereals (about 600,000 metric tons a year), with fertilizers a bad second, and organic chemical products a limping third. While trade in agricultural products and in the means to grow them may well continue at high levels for years to come, it is clearly in the French interest to buttress their commercial position in China with industrial goods the demand for which is likely to be less unpredictable, and in which France has a slight competitive edge.

The trouble with sales to China is that the Chinese are apparently not overburdened with foreign exchange. However, though China's precise foreign-exchange situation remains a closely guarded military secret, a careful study of Peking's Hong Kong, Macao, Ceylon and Malaysia trade, and of China's net trade balance with Western Europe, would indicate that the situation is not desperate by long odds. And if worst comes to worst, there is always the possibility of exporting silver. Moreover, the Chinese have in recent years learned quickly the techniques of trade with highly developed countries—something, incidentally, that the Soviets in their autarchic state of mind failed for decades to do.

Capitalist imperialists, even of the intermediate-zone variety, suffer, or as the case may be benefit, from rapid changes in demand induced by huge advertising expenditures. An intermediate zoner is fickle in his tastes, and however degenerate his flippancy may look to Socialist fundamentalists, they have to live with it if they want grain and turbines. Naturally, this puts a strain on them; they must make exotic Oriental foods (e.g., frozen sweet pork, rose-colored rice wine "to help digestion and render you happy and refreshed"), labor over carved teak chests for the bourgeois, and carved ivory figures . . . , shake Mandarin cocktails, and weave bright kimonos of select silk for anyone who cares to wear them today and give them to the concierge tomorrow. The moral and physical cost of industrialization is high: the makers of silk kimonos dress in padded felt uniforms, and the packers of frozen kumquats fight hunger pains as best they can. The blue ants of Chinese socialism burrow under the intermediate zoner's frivolity.

Of course, Chinese toil would be of little commercial consequence without help from French officialdom. What is needed here is bank credit on a large and rising scale. Jacques Duhamel, a member of the French National Assembly and of the quasi-private organization in charge of the French technical exhibition in Peking, estimates that the China market currently represents for the West annual sales of some $700 million, of which France takes about $60 million. In the absence of American incursions into the market, France expects to raise her share to an annual $200 million worth of goods and technical services. This increase, not to speak of an expansion in total Chinese purchases from the West, presupposes the granting by France and other Western countries of substantial medium and long-term credits to cover

Peking's recurrent trade deficit in her dealings with France, Canada, Australia, Belgium, Italy and Argentina. French recognition of Communist China early in 1964 removed one major obstacle to the proposed extension of credit, while China's scrupulous settling of her debts, not only to the West but also to her Soviet and Eastern European trading partners, further encouraged moves in the direction of a more liberal credit policy. It is interesting that France's four nationalized banks were represented on the committee that initiated the 1964 French industrial exhibit in China, and that European (including French) banks have helped finance Chinese grain purchases in Argentina and elsewhere, almost certainly with the knowledge and approval (and possibly active support) of their governments.

Petroleum products as well as drilling and refinery equipment are high on the Chinese list of import priorities. Until the Sino-Soviet break, the U.S.S.R. and Rumania were duopolistic suppliers of these key goods to China. After the break, Albania emerged as a petroleum seller, but the relatively low quality of its crude oil, the strain which transport put on hard-pressed Chinese shipping, and—in the absence of Soviet capital-goods exports to Albania— the uncertain future of the Albanian crude-oil industry, made Sino-Albanian relations in this sector a matter of political good will rather than a sound economic proposition.

The emergence of Algeria as an independent power favorably disposed toward Communist China and the regularization of Sino-French diplomatic relations converged to remove some of the pressure from the Chinese oil dilemma. At the same time, misunderstanding within the Soviet-sponsored Council for Mutual Economic Aid (Comecon) made Rumania more attentive to Chinese offers. The Rumanians had never taken kindly to Soviet pressures for something resembling an economic boycott of dissident China. Continued sales of petroleum products are for Rumania a matter of domestic importance, and perfectly correlated with the Rumanian leadership's maverick interpretation of Communist developmental strategy. China's current production of crude oil is estimated at between 6 and 8 million tons per annum (the higher figure being Chinese, the lower Comecon's), and consumption needs are nearer 10 million tons. In the midst of the Sino-Indian conflict, the Soviets cut off their exports of high-grade petroleum products to China, and Rumania's sales fell from about 1 million tons in 1963 to a mere 400,000 tons in 1964, in spite of Rumanian fretting. It would appear that for Rumania some of the sting was taken out of what, after all, was pure political blackmail on the part of the Soviets by the prospect of increased Rumanian petroleum sales to Italy. For China, however, the problem remained intense. The Chinese are nowadays boasting that they are "substantially" self-sufficient in oil, but if true this may reflect a temporary moratorium on the ambitious industrialization plans of the giddy fifties.

China needs not only petroleum products now, but refinery equipment in the future, and France stands ready to supply both, either directly (equipment) or through Algeria (oil). The main obstacle to the execution of the project consists in the modalities of payment. A triangular arrangement, whereby France would extend credit to Algeria for the purchase of Chinese goods in exchange for oil, cannot be excluded as a probable subject of Chou En-lai's conversations with Ben Bella [the Algerian leader, since ousted—Ed.] in Algiers, Edgar Faure's talks with Mao Tse-tung in Peking, the Chinese Petroleum and Natural Gas Production and Treatment delegation's four-week visit to France in the early months of 1964, and a return visit to China by a team of French petroleum experts in November of that year. A frequently mentioned estimate of China's petroleum import needs puts these at about 3 million tons per year. A consortium of French firms has been assiduously bidding for a contract to build an oil refinery in China, and contracts for the sale of exploration equipment were concluded late last year.

One of the costs involved in Peking's prolonged dependence on Soviet imports has been the lack of expertise on the part of Chinese negotiators in dealing on the international markets. This was particularly evident in the market for ship charters, where for some years the Chinese had been getting less than the best rates. The 1963 entry of the Soviet Union into the market for charter shipping to carry wheat bought in Canada, the United

States and elsewhere has made matters more difficult for the Chinese, whose own cargo fleet is both modest and relatively antiquated. To transport the grain purchased overseas, the Chinese had been obliged to charter more than 2 million tons of shipping at a most unpropitious time. They began to fight the problem in 1957-58 by purchasing a considerable number of World War II bottoms and by speeding up loading and unloading operations in their major ports. China's shipbuilding was put on a priority footing while efforts were made to find ship suppliers in the West.

In this case the timing was opportune since shipyards in Britain, France, the Netherlands, Japan and the Scandinavian countries had been in the doldrums for some years. Without new orders, [the shipyards at] St. Nazaire, La Ciotat and Dunkerque could well become centers of political opposition to Gaullism, just as Glasgow and Hull have turned sour on Britain's Conservatives. The Chinese, in the meantime, have learned their lesson well: a French delegation of shipbuilders that visited Peking in March 1964, found the Chinese hard and astute bargainers. Competitive offers from Japan were mentioned in passing, a reference which sent the Frenchmen scurrying back to their government with urgent appeals for credit guarantees. The Chinese have also developed a keen sense of political timing. In September of . . . [1964], the Toulon Forges et Chantiers de la Méditerranée shipyards announced that as of November 1, almost four hundred workers would be laid off. While 15,000 people were staging a silent vigil at the yards to protest this measure, Peking announced that it was ready to buy two 16,000 dwt. [dead-weight-ton] freighters, one of them from the afflicted shipyard. The Chinese also let it be known that they planned to order a liner from the St. Nazaire dockyards.

The precipitous decline in Sino-Soviet trade since 1960 has caused the Chinese serious land and air transportation problems, not to mention the frustration resulting from the grounding of China's Soviet-built combat planes. In spite of rising grain imports from abroad, China continues to rely heavily on her inland grain production to feed the populous coastal cities; and in the absence of an adequate road network, rail freight is of paramount importance in carrying out this task. The French are in a position to supply railroad cars and engines, as well as small agricultural machinery, which could be used with good effect on the farms of the coastal region, thus relieving somewhat the hard-pressed hinterland and the overworked trunk railroad lines. Since 1957, China has purchased 665 Berliet trucks from the French company's Moroccan and Algerian subsidiaries.

In the face of strong British competition, the French have been pushing hard to sell about thirty de-Americanized Caravelle jet air liners to the Chinese, whose interest in entering international air transport is growing. Most versions of the Caravelle are equipped with American engines, automatic pilot, pressurized systems and some other ancillary equipment. The United States embargo on exports to Communist China thus presents the French with a delicate political and technical problem. The difficulty, of course, is not insuperable, given the readiness of several European suppliers (e.g., Rolls Royce) to step into the breach. The manufacture of the Caravelle has been losing money; a sale of some thirty of these craft to China would get the Sud Aviation Company out of the red. When the Caravelle deal fell through, almost at once, the French began thinking about sales to China of the Franco-British Concord supersonic jet liner; the British, who aren't sure whether they want to go through with the joint arrangement anyway, became apprehensively alert.

Whatever the rationalization of France's economic relations with Communist China in cultural and pseudo-ideological terms (M. Courbot, president of the Paris Chamber of Commerce and Industry, spoke recently of France's "sentimental" ties to China), France's immediate domestic economic interest takes precedence. The French have been both quick and relatively successful in securing a foothold in a market from which, for different reasons, the world's two leading powers have shied away. Not unlike the Albanians, they also enjoy the psychological satisfaction of having snubbed big brother.

GENERAL DE GAULLE AND VIETNAM [4]

No one else, it would appear—not even Pope Paul VI or [UN Secretary General] U Thant—is better placed than Charles de Gaulle to help bring about a negotiated settlement in Vietnam. But the appearance is deceptive: as an arbitrator, de Gaulle has the power of a mailbox (which is not to say that mailboxes are useless). Justifiably, a New York *Times* editorial . . . points out that the general's advice on Vietnam might carry more weight today, if twenty years earlier his government had not sent to Indochina an expeditionary corps that, after 1954, had to be relieved by another army.

The sending of that armada headed by General Leclerc in the spring of 1945 was not motivated by purely colonial ambitions. By March 9, 1945, the Japanese had taken over Indochina; previously they had had only garrisons authorized by Vichy. Thus, the mission of the original French expeditionary corps was to "liberate" Vietnam from the Japanese rather than to reconquer it (this, at any rate, was the opinion then of the young French officers, including this writer). In its Declaration of March 24, 1945, de Gaulle's government offered the Vietnamese a somewhat vague system of self-government—a gesture that did not satisfy Ho Chi Minh's Vietminh propaganda for total independence.

Hiroshima spared the French expeditionary forces from having to fight the Japanese. But Hiroshima found the Vietminh entrenched in Hanoi and Saigon. Leclerc, regarded as de Gaulle's favorite disciple, quickly grasped that the Vietminh-inspired revolutionary movement had deep roots in the country and was not likely to be crushed militarily. Leclerc landed in Haiphong, went to Hanoi and negotiated with Ho Chi Minh the recognition of Vietnam as "a free state . . . within the French Union." He then cabled Paris that the word "independence" would be required to make the agreement stick.

However, besides Leclerc, the military commander-in-chief, de Gaulle had also appointed Admiral d'Argenlieu as "civilian"

[4] From article by Jean Lacouture, French journalist and author. *New Republic.* 154:19-21. Mr. 12, '66. Reprinted by permission of *The New Republic.* © 1966, Harrison-Blaine of New Jersey, Inc.

high commissioner to Vietnam and he outranked Leclerc. D'Argenlieu . . . promptly undid Leclerc's diplomatic work. In Saigon, he proclaimed an Autonomous Republic of Cochin China (South Vietnam), whereas under the agreement signed with Ho Chi Minh, its fate was to have been decided through a referendum. Provocative acts on both sides finally led to war.

General de Gaulle was not called upon publicly to choose between Leclerc's peace and d'Argenlieu's war, for in January 1946 he was no longer in power. We know, however, that the general did nothing to help Leclerc uphold his agreements policy; neither did he disavow d'Argenlieu when he, in turn, invoked de Gaulle's authority. When I returned from Indochina in early 1947, I went to see André Malraux, already one of the general's intimates. The strategy he outlined that day as being General de Gaulle's was exactly what [U.S.] General Gavin has just suggested—enclaves: "Hold the harbors, a few populated areas and wait. . . ." While the Indochina war lasted, de Gaulle's attitude remained the same; he criticized the governments of the Fourth Republic for the manner in which they waged the fight, rather than for waging it at all.

But from 1954 on, de Gaulle took a different position; he came to regard the war as foolish and as counter to France's vital interests in Europe and Africa. He therefore approved the results of the negotiations conducted in Geneva by [Premier] Mendès-France in July 1954. He even let his approval be known publicly, an extremely rare occurrence in view of his attitude toward the "regime of the parties." His lieutenants at the time . . . defended the agreements in Parliament. Jean Sainteny, a fervent Gaullist, was sent to Hanoi to represent France. As Leclerc's associate, he had negotiated with Ho the short-lived agreements.

When de Gaulle returned to power in 1958, Algeria and other colonial problems were so pressing that he seemed to take no interest in Indochinese affairs. French presence there was minimal anyway. The North Vietnamese government, behaving in a most doctrinaire and unpolitic manner, had no use for foreign capital. In the South, Ngo Dinh Diem was steering his government in a rather anti-French direction. When M. Pinay, then de Gaulle's finance minister, went to South Vietnam in November 1959 to try to improve relations between Saigon and Paris, de Gaulle merely tolerated the trip. He did nothing to exploit politically the détente Pinay had promoted by giving the Vietnamese a share in France's postcolonial interests in South Vietnam. The general stubbornly refused to receive Diem (during a trip to Europe Diem was planning on the occasion of a religious celebration), or to receive his brother Mr. Nhu. He regarded them both as "American agents" and found their rigid Catholicism absurd.

Nor did de Gaulle in 1963 encourage his ambassador in Saigon, M. Lalouette, a sincere friend of Mr. Nhu, to promote contacts between Saigon and the National Liberation Front, contacts that were then possible. The very discreet soundings taken by Lalouette (made public by Mr. Nhu in an interview a few weeks before his removal from power) were regarded as rash at the Élysée: why take such pains to save a dying and unfriendly regime?

Yet oddly enough, Diem's fall was by no means welcomed in Paris, except by the liberal press. For weeks General de Gaulle refused to recognize the new regime in Saigon, although it was headed at first by openly pro-French officers like Duong Van Minh, Lé Van Kim and Tran Van Don. Possibly he thought that for French-trained officers, these young men were singularly ill-bred or clumsy: to overthrow Diem was all right, but killing him was a different matter.

In any case, General de Gaulle had in mind more than some minor French cultural and economic interests in a small Asian country. Three months earlier, on August 29, 1963, he had made a declaration that stirred Hanoi as much as Washington and that can be summed up as follows: The Vietnamese conflict is political, not military, and it is by political means that it must be settled. The best way is to stop all foreign intervention and let the Vietnamese work out a solution among themselves, together with their Cambodian and Laotian neighbors. The word "neutralization" was not uttered, despite statements to the contrary, but it was the underlying idea and it was reiterated on many later occasions.

The Hope That Failed

From then on, General de Gaulle took a keen interest in the Vietnamese problem. He saw that in Hanoi and even in Peking his appeal had been well received; the French Embassy established in Peking would make contacts and thus negotiations easier. The scope of the soundings made by the general's emissaries and representatives has been overestimated; nevertheless, it was believed at the Élysée from the end of 1963 till February 1965 that Hanoi might be induced to negotiate and that neither the Vietcong nor Peking would completely block the way.

The best opportunity to start peace talks, so de Gaulle thought, was the Indochinese Peoples' Conference scheduled to open in February 1965 in Pnompenh, Cambodia. Three months earlier, Dr. Pham Ngoc Thach, the Hanoi government's minister of health, a personal friend of Ho Chi Minh and the former Vietminh leader in the South (his birthplace) had made an encouraging trip to Paris, and his later contacts at various levels (made with U Thant's help) had given UN circles some hope. The close relations between Prince Sihanouk and General de Gaulle, the "Indochinese" setting of the February 1965 conference, the then recent election of Lyndon B. Johnson all seemed to be good omens for negotiations.

Assuming that the Communist camp was seeking a way to avoid peace talks, it found an excuse in the start of United States bombings of the North on February 7, just when the Pnompenh Conference opened. General de Gaulle's hopes were thwarted, and his position on Indochina all through 1965 grew increasingly pessimistic, as did his bitterness toward Washington. . . . He regarded the resumption of the bombings and particularly its timing a few hours before the opening of the UN debate—a debate fraught with risks in any event—as an unprecedented strategic mistake. . . .

Even before the resumption of United States bombing of the North, however, the general had reason for pessimism. His last two emissaries to Asia, André Malraux and Jean Chauvel, had reported their doubts as to Peking's willingness to refrain from vetoing negotiations that would enable Washington to find an honorable way out. In Hanoi, Mr. Chauvel, who had been one of the main French negotiators in Geneva, was well received by Prime Minister Pham Van Dong. He left with the impression that if the North Vietnamese had the final say, talks would be possible, provided the bombings of the North stopped indefinitely and there were a "de-escalation" of the war in the South. But there remained the negative attitude of Peking and of the Vietcong.

Why has France been exerting its subtle influence in an area from which she seemed to have been eliminated and where she has no strong political leverage? There are French economic interests in Vietnam (Terres Rouges plantation, Michelin, etc., as well as industrial enterprises like the Indochina breweries and ice plants), but they belong to the postcolonial era, and de Gaulle has shown elsewhere, for instance in Algeria, that he cares little about the French *colons* and French private interests. His sly pleasure in teaching Washington a "lesson" is a different matter: he would like nothing better than to give the United States government grounds for gratitude to him. What matters to him above everything else is the enhancement of France's position in the world; he wishes to give her a brilliant role in peace, in a region where she had been humiliated. He wants to win over the noncommitted nations that are eager for the war to end. He seeks an active part in a major international drama, one in which political experience may be of great help, and where French culture—even if not a vital factor—is, nevertheless, a political asset.

IV.   FRANCE AND THE WESTERN ALLIANCE

EDITOR'S INTRODUCTION

The de Gaulle years have had a dramatic, if not fatal, impact on the Atlantic alliance. Prior to his coming to power, few in the United States or Europe questioned the continued need for NATO; nor did many doubt the desirability of United States leadership within the Western alliance. It was also widely assumed that the nations on both sides of the Atlantic were entering an age of increased cooperation and that allied relations would become progressively closer in the political and economic fields. The French president has shattered all of these beliefs.

De Gaulle, for reasons he considers perfectly valid, does not regard a United States-dominated NATO as a military force on which Europe can necessarily rely. While he considers himself an ally of the United States, he believes that United States dominance in the alliance threatens to submerge the European identity. Nor does he accept any form of political or economic integration if it involves the slightest surrender of national sovereignty. Thus, the hopes of those who believed the Common Market would set the stage for some form of political federation have been thwarted.

The articles in this section focus on the effect de Gaulle has had on the Atlantic alliance and on the movement toward European integration—though it should be noted that other factors, too, have played an important role in Common Market and alliance troubles. The first selection, published by the Foreign Policy Association, reviews the events which led to the formation of the alliance and details the evolution of the so-called Grand Design, the plan for a greater Atlantic Community. The next article recalls the strategic debate and presents the case for the French national nuclear force.

The Senate address by Senator J. William Fulbright represents a widely held point of view toward de Gaulle and his policies. The next articles deal with recent French actions toward NATO. Though still formally a member of the North Atlantic Treaty Organization, in practice France is no longer an active participant. The last two articles offer a broad perspective of de Gaulle and the future of Europe.

WESTERN EUROPE AND THE UNITED STATES [1]

The Atlantic alliance is experiencing a time of deep troubles. Current differences among its members mirror more than the normal disagreements to be expected even among close friends. Disunity in the allied camp runs broad and deep on a number of key issues. Many observers—both in this country and Western Europe—are wondering, therefore, whether the alliance can survive and, if so, for how long and in what shape.

The policies advocated and pursued by French President Charles de Gaulle provide the most dramatic evidence of distress in the alliance. President de Gaulle is attempting to create a French-led European third force which would constitute a center of strength independent of both the United States and the Soviet Union. The French leader has, simultaneously, thrown up roadblocks in the path of European economic integration and rejected efforts to move Europe toward closer political unity and transatlantic partnership.

It would be an oversimplification, however, to attribute Atlantic disunity exclusively to the policies of de Gaulle. On a variety of matters involving economics, German reunification, Western defenses, European integration and attitudes toward Moscow and Peking, the allies are rarely able to present a united front. The North Atlantic Treaty Organization (NATO), the military bulwark of the alliance, is divided over the problem of whose finger should be on the nuclear trigger. And two NATO

[1] From *Great Decisions 1966.* (Fact Sheet no. 3. Western Europe and the United States—End of the Atlantic Alliance?) Foreign Policy Association. 345 E. 46th St. New York 10017. '66. p 29-33. Copyright 1966 by the Foreign Policy Association, Inc. Reprinted by permission.

members, Greece and Turkey, are embroiled in a dispute over the future of Cyprus.

Nor do the allies always see eye to eye on questions which go beyond Atlantic concern. De Gaulle is critical of United States involvement in Vietnam. Our European allies were less than enthusiastic about Washington's intervention in the Dominican Republic. They have refused to accept the United States position that trade with such openly aggressive Communist nations as China, North Vietnam and Cuba should be embargoed.

To a generation of Americans accustomed to regarding the Atlantic alliance as the most enduring accomplishment of postwar United States foreign policy and as one of the indispensable necessities of international life, the current disarray among the Western nations comes as a shock. Why and how did it happen? Can it be checked and can Atlantic unity be restored? Is an Atlantic alliance necessary in terms of our vital interests? And above all—what kind of United States relationship with Western Europe is desirable and possible?

Out of the Ashes

The postwar Atlantic alliance was born in the desperate period after the defeat of Germany, when Europe lay devastated, vulnerable to Communist subversion and virtually defenseless against the threat of Soviet invasion. Responding to these dangers in its newly assumed role as free world leader, the United States initiated a series of imaginative and successful moves. In 1947 President Harry S. Truman asked Congress for some $400 million to help the Greek government combat a Communist-led guerrilla war and to assist Turkey in bolstering its defenses. The United States poured more than $13 billion into Marshall Plan economic aid for Western Europe, enabling that area to recover from the destruction of war and to reach or exceed prewar production levels by 1951.

In 1949, after a Communist coup had turned Czechoslovakia into a Soviet satellite and while West Berlin was still being blockaded by Moscow, the United States, Canada and ten

Western European countries signed the North Atlantic Treaty. The treaty—representing an unprecedented peacetime commitment for the United States—bound its signatories to regard an attack against one or more of them as an attack against all.

As soon as the member nations had ratified the treaty, they set about creating NATO, which is the organization responsible for carrying out the treaty's clauses and which provides for the integrated defense of the North Atlantic area under a unified command. In 1955 West Germany became a member of NATO, bringing the number of its participants to fifteen. (Greece and Turkey had joined in 1952).

Toward the Grand Design

The coordinated planning required to implement these programs helped lower traditional national barriers in Europe. Those on both sides of the Atlantic who long dreamed of European unification thought the time was ripe for a concerted drive toward that goal. A unified Western Europe, they believed, would help halt the suicidal continental wars which had periodically turned neighbor against neighbor. Unification would stimulate economic growth by enlarging markets and would also add appreciably to over-all Western security against the menace of Soviet expansionist drives. In this instance, the whole would be greater than the sum of its individual parts.

The late 1940's and the 1950's saw the birth of a number of cooperative ventures whose purpose was to build closer ties among the nations of Western Europe. Among the more important were the European Coal and Steel Community, Euratom (which was concerned with the joint development of atomic energy for peaceful purposes) and the enormously successful six-nation European Economic Community, popularly known as the Common Market—composed of France, West Germany, Italy, Belgium, the Netherlands and Luxembourg—which aimed at eliminating trade barriers among member nations as a step toward eventual political federation.

As the 1960's began, the architects and advocates of European union broadened their horizons and spoke of an Atlantic Community in which nations on both sides of the ocean would move toward common goals. Britain, which had originally preferred to stay out, began to negotiate for entry into the Common Market. And in a speech in Philadelphia in July 1962, President John F. Kennedy sketched the broad outlines of a new relationship that might develop between the United States and a united Western Europe, including Britain. He spoke of an interdependence among the nations of the Western world and of forming a concrete Atlantic partnership. He suggested that such a partnership might be composed of two equal parts: on the one hand, the United States and probably Canada; on the other, a united Western Europe. The goals of this Grand Design, as it was known, would be: (1) to create a strong, harmonious and prosperous Atlantic Community; (2) to contain communism and ultimately bring about its mellowing or retreat; and (3) to promote world economic growth by lowering trade barriers and helping the underdeveloped nations emerge from poverty.

A Dream Shattered

The vision of the Atlantic nations marching toward the fulfillment of the Grand Design has been rudely shattered in the last few years. "Washington's splendid plans, the Kennedy Grand Design, the concept of a Western Europe united and then twinned forever with the United States—all that is over," one U.S. journalist wrote. If many policy-makers in Washington or in Western Europe would still refuse to subscribe to this pessimistic conclusion, few could find much cause for optimism in the present state of Atlantic relations.

The malaise stems from a number of sources. But fundamentally the assorted ailments from which the alliance is suffering reflect a world situation that has radically changed in the last fifteen years and in which old relationships are not always compatible with new realities. In a sense, the alliance is the victim of its success in achieving its original aims: to foster the recovery and protect the security of Western Europe. As a result, the continued need for the alliance and the dominant role of the United States in it have come increasingly into question.

During the early postwar years of Western Europe's economic weakness and military vulnerability, it was assumed that a Soviet attack might come at any moment and that only the United States could provide the necessary military strength to deter an attack or to defend Western Europe should it come. United States leadership of NATO was welcomed and United States policies toward Western Europe were, for the most part, unhesitatingly accepted. Western Europe, in fact, had little choice but to accept a dependent status, and no option but to rely on the benevolence of American intentions and the strength of United States military power.

On this side of the Atlantic it was natural to accept United States leadership of the alliance as a normal and permanent feature of the order of things—to assume that our own interests and those of our allies ran along identical paths and that what was good for this country was good for the entire Atlantic Community.

Whatever the truth of these assumptions, it is understandable that nations with their own proud histories should resent being "wards" of another country any longer than they have to. In any event, it is clear in retrospect that the dependence of Western Europe on the United States was the product of abnormal postwar conditions, and that it would begin to lessen once the area had regained its strength and the military danger from the Soviet Union had receded.

In the 1950's, as Western Europe moved toward prosperity and recovered its self-confidence, it began to speak with greater assertiveness. The death of Stalin, the weakening of the Soviet hold over Eastern Europe, the cold war relaxation in Europe and the periods of détente between Washington and Moscow encouraged this assertiveness by appearing to diminish the need for Atlantic unity and to lessen the risks of disunity. If the superpowers were willing to coexist; if, as some asserted, they had a common interest in preserving the status quo so as to decrease the dangers of a nuclear war, then Western Europe had room to maneuver and to free itself from too close a reliance on the United States.

Still another factor contributing to the strains on Atlantic unity was the global process of postwar decolonization. As the involvement of the former European colonial powers in the affairs of the new African and Asian nations weakened, the United States involvement increased. This development produced a different and sometimes conflicting scale of priorities among Atlantic nations. The United States, for example, has been dissatisfied by what it considers to be the reluctance of some of its European allies to carry their share of the foreign aid burden, while some of our allies have at times resented the anticolonial positions we have taken in the UN.

When the Kennedy Administration took office in 1961, United States policy-makers were aware that the original conditions which had created the need for the Atlantic alliance no longer prevailed and that the times called for a new approach to Atlantic unity. This, in fact, was the motivation for President Kennedy's speech outlining the Grand Design. Its purpose was to suggest the willingness of the United States to consider a modification of the alliance in the light of changing times and to inspire enthusiasm among our allies for a cooperative approach toward this task. However, although the speech was warmly received in most of Western Europe, particularly in West Germany, it failed to arouse any enthusiasm in President de Gaulle.

Today the Atlantic alliance faces an uncertain and problematic future. Many challenges confront it as a result of the policies of de Gaulle and allied differences over military, economic and political issues. What is the specific nature of these challenges? How can—and how should—they be met by the Atlantic allies? . . .

Two Views of Europe

Two major schools of thought on the subject of future European and Atlantic relationships dominate the contemporary scene. One school, variously known as integrationist, federalist and

Atlanticist, which probably includes a majority of concerned Europeans, favors a tightly knit Western European union bound by supranational ties. The Common Market was expected to mark a first step toward eventual political union.

In such a union, as this school envisages it, member nations would not lose their sovereignty in purely domestic matters, and the nation itself would not lose its identity. However, on major questions concerning Western Europe as a whole—initially in the economic field and later in foreign policy and defense—the separate countries would gradually develop common institutions that would ultimately pave the way for a European government and some form of European parliament.

The integrationists, to be sure, differ on matters of detail. Some, for instance, would have Europe develop its own independent nuclear force to be coordinated with the United States nuclear force. Others prefer that United States and European efforts be merged in a single deterrent, while still others contend that the nuclear facts of life require Europe to put itself under the protection of the United States. But all integrationists agree that European union is the desired goal and the prerequisite for full Atlantic partnership with the United States. A close identity of views exists between this school and Washington.

Enter de Gaulle. His views conflict, in no uncertain terms, with those of the integrationists. He and his followers—and there are Gaullists outside France, particularly in West Germany —believe that the nation-state is the basic force in international relations and that cooperation of sovereign governments leading toward a confederation is the best route to a "European Europe" —a Europe independent of and equal to the United States. Thus, de Gaulle maintains it is unthinkable for any great power to delegate its sovereignty to a supranational body or to subordinate its powers of decision even to the will of a majority of the nations with which it is allied. . . .

This does not mean de Gaulle opposes all forms of European or Atlantic alliance. He recognizes the stimulating economic benefits brought to France and Western Europe by the Common Market, and last September [1965] he declared to the world that

France will remain an ally of its allies so long as Western solidarity is "necessary for the possible defense of Europe." What de Gaulle specifically opposes is the principle of integration which the advocates of European union favor and the form of partnership which the United States and others in Europe have championed.

Integration leading to European political union is out of the question, de Gaulle maintains, since it would diminish French sovereignty. And were France to subscribe to American plans for partnership (which call initially for United States control of the West's nuclear defense), de Gaulle believes his country would be placing itself in perpetual dependency on Washington.

Gaullism in Action

Virtually all the policies de Gaulle has pursued toward Western Europe and the United States can be explained in terms of this general framework. He has withdrawn the French fleet and most French land forces from NATO because he is opposed to NATO's integrated command structure. He has refused to participate in NATO maneuvers . . . because they follow American strategic doctrines with which he disagrees.

In pursuit of his version of national independence, de Gaulle has developed his own small nuclear force, whose first elements are now operational. This *force de frappe* [striking force], as it is known, consisting of some fifty bombers capable of delivering nuclear bombs, is scheduled to be completed by 1967.

That such a delivery system may already be obsolescent does not deter de Gaulle. Nor does the fact that France is paying a tremendous price to build its nuclear arsenal, a price many believe it cannot really afford, sway de Gaulle's determination. He maintains that no really independent and industrialized nation can be expected to rely on the armaments of another nation. De Gaulle well knows he cannot match the nuclear might or the technological pace of the superpowers. But he is not interested in nuclear parity.

De Gaulle is confident that his national nuclear force, no matter how small, cannot be ignored. Within the next decade France may also build a submarine fleet capable of carrying Polaris-type missiles and may bury other missiles in hardened sites.

The destructive power of his *force de frappe* would be considerable, and it could hardly be ignored. Thus, de Gaulle reasons, France will have gained greater control over its destiny and will be afforded a more respected voice in Western military councils.

Shaking Up the Market

The most dramatic move de Gaulle has made since his return to office occurred in January 1963 when he abruptly vetoed a British bid for Common Market membership. [See "On Vetoing the British Common Market Application Bid," in Section II, above.] This jolting development shook integrationists and produced confusion among diplomats on both sides of the Atlantic.

As always, de Gaulle had his reasons. He claimed that Britain was not truly a European country; that its ties to the Commonwealth and the United States were closer and dearer to it than any of its bonds with Europe; and that British membership in the Common Market would give Washington too great an influence over European affairs.

Whether these contentions were true or not, a plausible case could be made to support them. Britain had originally remained aloof from the Common Market—in part because of trade commitments to the Commonwealth. It had even formed the Outer Seven free trade group (including, in addition to itself, Austria, Denmark, Norway, Portugal, Sweden and Switzerland) as a counter to the Common Market. Only when the success of the Common Market was too great to be ignored did Britain make its unsuccessful bid for membership. And in nuclear matters, Britain alone, of all our allies, shared some of the United States secrets —as a result of its original role in developing atomic energy.

Shortly after turning down the British Common Market application, de Gaulle signed a treaty of collaboration with West

Germany. It was his hope that this would provide a foundation for a Franco-German entente which would lead Europe in the years ahead. Although most Germans welcomed friendlier relations with France, de Gaulle was unsuccessful in weakening West Germany's ties with the United States. The Federal Republic still regards NATO and the United States commitment to it as the main prop in the country's protection against the threat of Soviet aggression.

Diplomatic Arrows

De Gaulle's diplomatic arrows have flown thick and fast, particularly in the last two years. He has spoken in vague terms of his hopes for a Europe from the Atlantic to the Urals, a possibility which could come to pass when and if Moscow gives up its present imperial designs and modifies its totalitarian internal system. In such a Europe, the problem of a divided Germany might be dealt with by the European nations primarily concerned, with the United States playing only a secondary role.

The French president has toured Latin America, where France has sizable private investments and cultural ties, and has offered French friendship and cooperation as a counterweight to Washington's dominant influence in the area. He has called for the neutralization of South Vietnam and has offered French assistance in mediating the Vietnamese conflict. He has recognized Communist China and increased trade with Cuba. He has refused to accept the authority of the UN General Assembly to levy peacekeeping assessments. He has advocated a return to the gold standard and converted substantial amounts of French dollar holdings into gold, asserting that the dollar no longer should enjoy a privileged status as a reserve currency. Finally, and most important of all, at his September 1965 press conference he indicated he will insist upon basic reforms in the structure of NATO when the North Atlantic Treaty expires in 1969. As he put it, "We shall end the subordination which is described as integration, which is provided for by NATO and which puts our destiny in the hands of foreigners."

Gaullism Without de Gaulle?

When de Gaulle first began to challenge prevailing conceptions regarding the future of Atlantic unity, many in high places in Western Europe and the United States refused to take the challenge seriously. The widespread view was that given the maverick he had always been, de Gaulle was merely trying to make his presence on the scene forcefully felt or was taking his revenge on the United States and Britain for alleged wartime slights to him and to French prestige. It was assumed that once de Gaulle had asserted himself and had made it clear that France would no longer compliantly say yes to the United States, he would become more "reasonable" and the differences between France and its allies would be reconciled.

But as the French leader threw up one roadblock after another in the path of the movement toward European and Atlantic unity, this assumption no longer seemed tenable. Some opponents of de Gaulle then hoped that because of his age, the French leader's tenure in office would be limited; and that once he disappeared from the scene, Gaullism as a factor in Atlantic affairs would also disappear. Then the trend toward European integration and Atlantic unity would move forward.

Today there is considerably less confidence that de Gaulle's . . . ultimate retirement from office would remove the challenge with which he is identified. For one thing, de Gaulle may be able to pick his successor, and that successor could be expected to follow many Gaullist policies. In addition, de Gaulle's insistence on the primacy of the nation-state as the enduring and indestructible agent in international affairs is a view that has much to support it in past history and in the present facts of international life.

THE STRATEGIC DEBATE [2]

During the early postwar years, when the threat of a Soviet attack on Europe appeared at its height, the West relied mainly

[2] From *Great Decisions 1966*. (Fact Sheet no. 3. Western Europe and the United States—End of the Atlantic Alliance?) Foreign Policy Association. 345 E. 46th St. New York 10017. '66. p 34-5. Copyright 1966 by the Foreign Policy Association, Inc. Reprinted by permission.

on the United States atomic bomb to deter the Communists. Indeed, many believed that only the fear of United States atomic retaliation kept the Soviet Union from marching to the English Channel. But reliance on atomic bombs posed such frightful prospects that the West, through NATO, turned to more conventional means of defense.

At first, the NATO powers set themselves a manpower goal of 60 to 90 divisions on the Central European front. But when it was obvious that the allies could not or would not meet this figure, the goal was reduced to 50 divisions. This figure could not be reached, and NATO finally settled for a 30-division plateau. Even this goal has never been achieved.

To compensate for its lack of manpower, NATO began to lean more heavily on United States tactical nuclear weapons, which were placed in several allied countries. As the generals plotted it on their maps, if the Soviet Union attacked, NATO's conventional forces would serve as a trip wire or plate glass window through which the Communists would have to crash. NATO troops would delay the Communists as long as possible and attempt to force the enemy into large concentrations. NATO's nuclear sword would then be ready to annihilate the foe.

However, as the Soviet Union perfected its own arsenal of tactical atomic weapons and then developed long-range missile delivery systems, the danger grew that any use of nuclear arms would lead to full-scale nuclear war. In a sense, the nuclear weapons of the superpowers canceled each other out in what became known as the balance of terror.

Flexible Response

When the Kennedy Administration took office in 1961, it sought a safety valve so that if war did erupt it would not necessarily lead to a nuclear Armageddon. It was the Administration's contention that the West had become too heavily dependent on nuclear weapons and was unprepared to meet a conventional attack on Europe without being quickly forced to resort to limited or all-out nuclear war.

The United States accordingly, invested heavily in a broadly based program for the development of all types of conventional weapons and methods of fighting. Washington also asked the allies to increase their troop levels so that the West's means of waging conventional war might be further augmented. The reasoning was that if the West were capable of a flexible type of response, it would not be compelled to resort to nuclear war just because it could wage no other kind of conflict effectively.

Flexible response would enable the allies to react in several ways, depending on the force required and the goals sought. The West could lash out with a crushing retaliatory blow; it could strike with nuclear weapons against selected targets; it could employ land troops or both conventional and nuclear means. Even if conventional means proved insufficient to halt the enemy, the war could be escalated gradually, perhaps even over the tactical nuclear threshold, but still beneath the level of all-out atomic holocaust.

Credibility Factors

Not all Europeans, however, are convinced that the strategy of flexible response offers the best answer to their military and security problems. As some see it, asking for an increase in European troops is asking for more fodder for the enemy cannons. If the superpowers fight a conventional war, they will probably fight it on European soil. While the United States might consider this preferable to a nuclear holocaust, a conventional conflict in Europe would spell disaster for Europeans. They might therefore prefer a direct nuclear exchange between the United States and the Soviet Union, since Europe would have at least a chance of avoiding destruction.

Some Europeans also worry about an apparent reversal of roles, in which the United States now refers to NATO's conventional forces as the sword and nuclear arms as the shield. Does this imply a United States reluctance to use nuclear arms for the defense of Europe?

In the European view the United States may have good reason for such hesitation. When the United States was immune from Soviet attack, in the days before Moscow had long-range missiles, Washington's pledges of military aid were perfectly credible. But now that the Soviet Union has a large array of intercontinental ballistic missiles targeted on the United States, Europeans say they cannot be so sure that Washington will risk destruction of this country if the Soviet Union should attack elsewhere.

Europeans have found still other grounds for questioning the reliability of the American commitment. If, for instance, the United States is able to alter its strategic doctrines unilaterally, might it not also unilaterally withdraw its pledges of protection? It has not passed unnoticed in Europe that a number of prominent Americans have called for a reduction in United States troops stationed in Europe—either to force the Europeans to make a greater defense effort, or to help correct the United States balance of payments deficit.

Many Europeans regard the United States troop presence as a hostage force, a guarantee of American commitment. To remove part of the hostage force would aggravate the fears of those who believe that the United States may retreat someday to a fortress America concept. Finally, valid and sincere as the American commitment may be today, Europeans say they cannot be sure that these guarantees will be binding on a President a decade hence.

Gaullists and others see one answer to these doubts. They claim that Europe's best course is to develop and control its own nuclear forces. Hence the *force de frappe;* hence a British nuclear deterrent, which, for all its ties to NATO, could be used independently.

The United States has never accepted the necessity for the development of independent nuclear forces outside of NATO. Washington argues that since its own forces already cover all conceivable targets there is no need for other nuclear forces; that national nuclear forces, such as the *force de frappe,* injure allied unity because they imply that the United States is not to be completely trusted; that national nuclear forces are wasteful, eat up resources that could be better utilized for other projects, promote nuclear proliferation and are too small and too vulnerable to be of genuine deterrent value.

The United States has tried to erase European doubts and insecurities by repeated protestations of support. "The United States will risk its cities to defend yours," President Kennedy said in 1963, "because we need your freedom to protect ours." President Johnson has reaffirmed this pledge on many occasions. So have Secretary of State Dean Rusk and other Administration officials. The United States has not retreated from West Berlin in the face of Soviet pressures; it has not withdrawn to a fortress America; its leaders continue to stress the close links between European and American security.

But perhaps the European countries have seen too many of the most solemn promises broken in the past not to fear that the American guarantee might evaporate in the future under the strain of a nuclear showdown. Perhaps, too, the need for military support is no longer vital in an age when many people in Western Europe discount the possibility of a Soviet attack and, as a result, see no compelling need to accept American military protection.

Multilateral Force

In any event, our NATO partners have been asking for a greater role in the command decisions regarding the West's deterrent nuclear force—which is really the deterrent force of the United States. In an effort to establish what it hoped would be an acceptable basis for nuclear partnership, the United States proposed that a multilateral force (MLF) of 25 surface vessels be formed, with most of the cost to be borne by the United States and West Germany, the two NATO countries best able to underwrite such expenses. Each ship would be armed with eight 2,500-mile-range Polaris missiles and manned by a mixed crew from at least three of the participating nations, including the United States. The fleet would operate on a unanimity principle, with each participant able to veto a decision to fire the missiles.

The United States saw many advantages in MLF. The legitimate allied request to share nuclear responsibility would be met, yet command would remain centralized for more reliable control. Neither de Gaulle nor any other ally would have to develop an independent force outside of NATO, and the danger of nuclear proliferation could be lessened. West Germany would be part of MLF, and the widespread fear that the Germans might embark on their own nuclear program would be quieted.

However, MLF did not receive an enthusiastic reception. France rejected the idea. Most other NATO countries were lukewarm, although some of them agreed to join the United States in further planning. Only West Germany endorsed MLF with any enthusiasm.

The multilateral force has been criticized on a number of grounds. Since MLF would form only a minute proportion of total Western nuclear strength, it was not worth the cost, according to some. MLF has been called "military nonsense" and, though feasible, strategically unnecessary. Some critics fear that MLF provides a back door through which West Germany can step to get its hands on nuclear weapons. But the basic objection to MLF is that the United States would still retain veto power over the use of the missiles and that the concept of shared responsibility, therefore, would be an illusion. As a result of these objections, the Johnson Administration appears to have shelved ... the MLF idea. . . .

Nuclear Options

A number of nuclear choices are open to the United States. Washington could try to convince Europe that its most practical course would be to place itself under our nuclear trusteeship. The United States could accept the nuclear nationalism of de Gaulle and not oppose the development of independent nuclear forces. Washington could revive MLF or put forth some other plan with a view toward integrating Atlantic nuclear forces. (Press reports last October declared that the United States was considering proposing the creation of a small nuclear planning committee within NATO as a way of giving our allies a nuclear voice yet halting the spread of nuclear weapons.) The possibility cannot be ruled out, for instance, that at some future date a French-British nuclear deterrent could take over primary responsibility for the defense of Europe. This force, presumably, could be coordinated with the United States nuclear force.

In his book, *The Troubled Partnership*, Professor Henry A. Kissinger of Harvard University outlines another version of nuclear integration. He recommends that an allied nuclear force be formed of United States, British and French units exclusively, with veto provisions built into any agreement. The force would be designed so as to operate according to the principles of flexible response. There would also be a "political mechanism to plan long-term policy, to manage crises and to control the nuclear weapons of the alliance."

Each choice, however, has it drawbacks and difficulties. Many Europeans are unwilling to leave their defenses permanently in our trust. Yet nuclear nationalism means nuclear proliferation, which has been called one of the greatest perils facing the world today. And any plan for an integrated nuclear alliance runs into Gaullist opposition.

FRANCE AND THE WESTERN ALLIANCE [3]

There is a tone of recrimination in General de Gaulle's remarks, of doubt and distrust as to the motives and objectives of American policy. It is this mistrust that disturbs France's partners and weakens the Atlantic alliance. It is important, therefore, that the suspicions that now divide us be discussed and debated in all their particulars, with a view toward restoring trust and confidence in the Western alliance. . . .

President de Gaulle [has] set forth certain basic principles that comport entirely with the views of the United States that "the fundamental factors of French-American relations are friendship and alliance"; that this friendship is "an outstanding psychological

[3] From "France and the Western Alliance: Actual Cooperation Is Needed," address by Senator James William Fulbright (Democrat, Arkansas), delivered in the United States Senate, October 29, 1963. Text from *Vital Speeches of the Day.* 30:75-8. N. 15, '63.

reality in keeping with the nature of the two countries"; that the Atlantic alliance is an "elemental necessity" and that within it France and the United States have a "capital responsibility."

These broad principles are as valid in content as they are eloquent in expression. President de Gaulle is also correct in warning us against "depicting each scratch as an incurable wound." At the same time, I think it appropriate for us to remind France and the other countries of Western Europe that a viable alliance depends on common policies as well as common objectives, on cooperation in fact as well as agreement in principle. If the Western alliance is to remain strong and united, it must be built on more than bonds of friendship and high regard. It requires working agreements for political consultation and the command and disposition of military forces, for economic cooperation and the lowering of trade barriers.

It is on this level of practical cooperation that French policy has been deeply disappointing to France's allies. It is a policy which, if long continued, could lead to the disruption of the Western alliance, not by open repudiation but by abnegation in detail.

In a meeting at Harvard University, . . . a distinguished young professor of politics told me that I had made what he called a "useful and necessary" effort to understand what is going on in the Soviet Union and he urged me to make a similar effort with regard to France. I believe this suggestion was entirely appropriate. It is certainly important for Americans to make an effort to understand the political, military and historical motivations of current French policy. It is no less important for France to make a commensurate effort with regard to the problems and objectives of American policy.

A meaningful dialogue between France and the United States must begin with an examination of the profound impact on both countries of the events of the last twenty-five years.

France, as President de Gaulle pointed out on July 29, was "materially and morally destroyed by the collapse of 1940" and by the discreditable Vichy interlude. Following the Liberation, France was beset by political and economic weaknesses at home and by the long and fruitless struggles in Indochina and Algeria. All this time France was forced into a relationship of military and economic dependence on the United States, a deeply humiliating experience for a great and proud nation. Since General de Gaulle's return to power in 1958, France, with astonishing speed, has recovered her political stability, ended the colonial wars, and returned to vibrant economic health.

As a result of this great resurgence, France has ended her economic dependency on the United States and reasserted herself with vigor and confidence as one of the great nations of Europe. These developments are as welcome to the United States as they are to France, but the memory of defeat and dependency remains and one perceives in current French policy an excess of pride and assertiveness that is entirely natural for a great nation which was struck down and has only recently recovered its dignity and strength. It is natural for France to be acutely sensitive and proud at this juncture in her history, and it is even natural for her to feel resentment toward those who liberated her and then sustained her through the years of weakness.

It is natural but it does not represent an accurate interpretation of the events of the last twenty years. The United States did not wish to become the protector and benefactor of Europe after World War II. Still less did it wish to dominate Europe. Through the Marshall plan and subsequent programs of military and economic support, America came to Europe's assistance for the simple but compelling reason that Europe was momentarily incapable of sustaining itself and its recovery was vital to the interests of the United States. America's postwar policy toward Europe was by no means an exercise in pure altruism but neither was it an effort to dominate Europe. It was a policy of enlightened mutual interest and its success has brought signal benefits to both Europe and America.

These elemental facts provide the basis for an accurate assessment of the motives and objectives of American policy. I do not believe that President de Gaulle is disposed at present to take such a dispassionate view of American policy. One perceives in his remarks . . . that he is still looking at America through the distorting prism of wounded pride.

This attitude is reflected in the General's comments on economic and trade relations and on the American balance-of-payments problem. He acknowledges that the United States is carrying a heavy burden of military and economic assistance to many countries and that the balance-of-payments and dollar problems of the United States have become essential concerns. One might have hoped that President de Gaulle would regard these problems as essential concerns of the entire alliance, which America's partners would wish to help alleviate. Instead, the general reasserted his hopes for a closed European economy.

France—he said—

cannot and does not wish to see the nascent economy of Europe and itself dissolved in a system of a type of Atlantic Community which would only be a new form of that famous integration.

Lest there be any doubt about his intentions with regard to trade, the general refers in his statement to "the storms which will not fail to come up" on the occasion of the "Kennedy round" of tariff negotiations scheduled for next spring [1964].

General de Gaulle points with justifiable pride to the restoration of France's currency, finances, and trade, without in any way suggesting that France might wish to make a greater contribution to the defense and security of the Western alliance. Not only has France recovered its economic independence but, in the General's words:

It finds itself receiving requests from many sides, and so, far from borrowing from others, particularly from the Americans, it is paying back its debts to them and even on occasion is granting them certain facilities.

If we wish to reply to President de Gaulle in a spirit as generous as his own, we might remind him of France's total unpaid debt to the United States of $6,340,164,589.32 deriving from World War I loans, of which $4,317,161,803.19 in principal and interest was due and unpaid as of June 30, 1963. The payment of this debt, on which France has been in default since June 1933, would unquestionably alleviate the American balance-of-payments deficits which the general concedes is an "essential concern."

The United States has not demanded payment of the World War I debts of France and other European countries. We have not demanded payment of these debts because we recognize, as we did not thirty years ago, that the war of 1914 was our war as well as France's, and that now, as then, the defense of the West must be a unified and cooperative endeavor in which each partner contributes in proportion to its resources. Our acceptance of the common obligations of the Western partnership was demonstrated with wisdom and success in the Marshall plan, which provided substantial grants for which repayment was neither required nor expected.

I emphasize the point that under the Marshall plan more than half of the amount which was given to France was in outright grants, for which France never undertook any obligation to repay. Incidentally, they received the largest amount, I believe, of any single country in continental Europe in the form of both grants and loans. However, the debt to which I referred that occurred during and after World War I was an obligation which they did assume and which they have never discharged.

This spirit of common interest and common obligation is strikingly lacking in current French policy. Like America in the inter-war period, France seems to believe that it has the option to participate or abstain from the projects of the alliance as it may suit France's peculiar preferences or ambitions. Just as America in the twenties demanded payment of the Allied war debts and then made payment impossible by high tariff barriers which prevented Europe from earning the dollars with which to pay, France now expresses sympathy and concern for the heavy financial burdens of the United States and proceeds to aggravate these burdens by seeking to exclude American goods from a closed European market.

Should France decide before next spring to join with her Atlantic partners in a general liberalization of trade, the way will be open to generate new levels of prosperity and accelerated economic growth in both Europe and America. Instead of the current tendency toward trade restrictions on one side followed by retaliation on the other, we can enter a new cooperative relationship, one which will alleviate the strains that now divide us and greatly strengthen the economic base of the Western partnership. . . .

Another theme of President de Gaulle's . . . that is disappointing to France's partners is his reassertion of the view that America cannot be counted upon to meet its obligations in the defense of Europe. Because of the loss of the American nuclear monopoly and the acquisition by the Soviet Union of the power to devastate the American continent, the United States, in General de Gaulle's view, "is seeing its own survival as the principal objective in a possible conflict and is not considering the time, degree, terms, and conditions of its nuclear intervention for the defense of other regions, particularly Europe, except in relation to this natural and primary necessity." This assumption is the foundation of the general's conviction that France must build an independent nuclear arsenal. The alliance must be modified, he says, because, as he puts it, it "has been built on the basis of integration, which is no longer valid for us."

The assumption that the United States might stand aside while Europe is devastated and overrun is patently unfounded. In both word and deed, the United States has committed itself unalterably to the defense of Europe—by its adherence to the NATO treaty, by innumerable declarations and reassurances, and by the presence in the heart of Europe of 400,000 American troops. I do not know what further assurances would be required to persuade General de Gaulle that we intend to honor our obligations.

But even if these commitments are set aside, it is inconceivable from a strategic point of view that the United States would stand aside—or that the Soviet Union would permit it to stand aside—while Western Europe was overrun. A third world war could not possibly follow the pattern of 1914 and 1939 in which France was attacked while the United States remained temporarily unscathed behind its ocean barriers. . . .

Nor is it possible to imagine that the Russians would take the incredible risk of leaving the United States out of the conflict with its forces intact and able to intervene whenever it chose.

If anything at all can be regarded as certain about a possible nuclear war, it is that the outcome of such a conflict would be determined not in Western Europe but in the two great centers of nuclear power, in Russia and the United States.

We are dealing here in possibilities not certainties, but so is General de Gaulle. His strategic concept, as I see it, is one of preparing for the least likely contingency, that of a Communist attack on Western Europe from which the United States would be permitted and would choose to stand aside. It seems far more likely, if there is any rationality in Soviet strategic doctrine, that the reverse situation might occur, an assault on the United States from which Europe would be spared.

The overwhelming probability is that neither Europe nor America would be spared devastation in a nuclear war. In the two world wars, the Western nations paid a grievous price for the illusion held by some of them that security could be found in isolation. We Americans have learned the costly lesson of our isolationism. It is our hope that our partners, who suffered far more grievously than we from the disunity of the past, will not be tempted to experiment with disunity again, because its price has become unpayable and few would survive to profit from the lesson.

For these reasons it is essential that Europe, including France, commit itself to a unified defense of the West. Europe can and should make a far greater contribution to the alliance than it is now making. The United States at present is putting 11 per cent of its gross national product into defense and foreign aid, while some of its allies are doing less than half as much proportionately. The United States, which has committed itself to a unified defense of the West, will not of its volition abandon Europe, but this does not mean that it cannot be driven from Europe. If our partners pursue protectionist trade policies and decline to carry a proportion of the military and foreign aid burdens commensurate with their resources, the United States will be left with no choice but to reduce its commitments. General de Gaulle considers American withdrawal from Europe inevitable. It is not inevitable —unless Europe makes it so.

The necessary complement of a greater European contribution to the alliance is a greater European voice in its vital decisions. Europe can and should be brought into the strategic planning processes which govern the use of America's nuclear arsenal. A unified strategic planning system, aimed at the development of a strategic consensus among the allies, can be developed within the existing framework of NATO. The NATO Council, which has not played the significant role envisioned for it by the framers of the treaty in 1949, could now be developed into an allied strategic planning body on the model of the combined Chiefs of Staff of World War II. It could become the allied forum for long-termed political and military planning on the most fundamental questions of war and peace.

As Alastair Buchan, the Director of Britain's Institute for Strategic Studies, recently pointed out:

The beginning of a solution to the problems of command and control of nuclear weapons lies in making the European allies partners in the Washington debate from which emerge policies on arms control, for the defense of Europe and for meeting the world-wide responsibilities of the United States. If the multilateral process is insufficient for all purposes, there are few people in Europe who would not welcome the deliberate cultivation of a "special relationship" between France and the United States. [Alastair Buchan, "Partners and Allies," *Foreign Affairs,* July 1963, p. 657.]

The final theme . . . on which I wish to comment is that of France's attitude toward the nuclear test ban treaty. General de Gaulle states that the treaty was negotiated by the Soviets and the "Anglo-Saxons," "in the absence of the Europeans, which clearly goes against the views of France." It hardly needs to be pointed out that the Europeans were absent only because France chose to absent herself.

The test ban treaty, said General de Gaulle, . . . has "only limited practical importance" in that "it in no way alters the terrible threat that the nuclear weapons of the two rivals bring to bear on the world." In a subsequent statement . . General de Gaulle suggested that universal acceptance of the test ban treaty would constitute an agreement that "two privileged states should hold forever the monopoly of power," thereby "delivering the world to a double hegemony." . . .

Whatever merit there may be in General de Gaulle's views on disarmament—and there may be great merit in them—one recognizes in his manner of expressing them the same wounded pride and aloofness that characterizes his views on so many other matters. This is, of course, disappointing to France's partners, who want her participation in their negotiations and decisions, both within the alliance and in their relations with the Soviet Union. But it is hardly reasonable to expect the members of the alliance to put the major issues of the decade on ice while France completes the process of recovering her full measure of strength and pride—including, perhaps, a sizable nuclear arsenal. . . .

For too long France's voice has been a voice of negation and dissent within the Western community. The alliance has suffered for lack of the constructive counsel of one of its greatest and most creative members. Only when France has resumed her rightful place in the alliance will its affairs be in order. Only then will we have advanced in the useful and necessary effort toward understanding on which our security and welfare depend.

AMI, GO HOME [4]

There may be a mystical streak in Charles de Gaulle, but there is little mystery in his policy. Ever since returning to power eight years ago, he has been trying to drive the same point home to Washington. France must share in the big decisions. First, he proposed to President Eisenhower the establishment of a triumvirate—the United States, Britain and France—which would more or less run the affairs of the Western world and manage the cold war. That proposal was met initially with contemptuous silence; then, somewhat later, with a flat no. The

[4] From "De Gaulle's Moves Against NATO Have a Long History: Ami, Go Home," by Philip Ben, free-lance writer. *New Republic.* 154:10-11. Ap. 9, '66. Reprinted by permission of *The New Republic,* © 1966, Harrison-Blaine of New Jersey, Inc.

theme was repeated when John Kennedy came to the White House, and for a brief time it looked as if the young and energetic President, receptive to new ideas, might meet the general halfway. But Mr. Kennedy's advisers decided that, after all, France was a "negligible quantity," that it was sheer arrogance for de Gaulle to demand equal status with the all-powerful United States. The project for a multilateral force, conceived in the Kennedy era, was considered by Paris as having only one object: the isolation of France in Western Europe and the strengthening of United States hegemony. From the French point of view, Kennedy's triumphal visit to Germany was made chiefly to off-set the impression of de Gaulle's visit some nine months earlier.

When Lyndon Johnson assumed the presidency, de Gaulle bided his time, for a bit. When hints began arriving from Paris that the general was impatient to begin discussions about the future, there was no response, and soon thereafter de Gaulle shifted his tactics. He would act so that Washington could not ignore him; he would engage in nuisance diplomacy. This was the period of bitter recriminations, of harsh statements by de Gaulle and his lieutenants about American policy. It was the time of de Gaulle's own unprecedented tour of South America, of French anti-American initiatives in the United Nations, of de Gaulle's recognition of Communist China. Johnson remained unimpressed.

Now we are witnessing the beginning of Act III. De Gaulle no longer threatens. Instead, last week in Paris he tells Under-secretary of State George Ball that he hopes that the NATO headquarters and American and Canadian military bases will have left French soil within a year; and he lets it be known that French forces in West Germany will be withdrawn from NATO by July. It is as if he were saying: "I tried to persuade you to agree to a true partnership. That was rejected. Now you will begin to feel that you need France more than you believed you would; there are many things you wish to do which will become outright impossible if we stand firmly against you." De Gaulle's frustrations . . . have been aggravated by several other factors. For instance, the general frequently refers to "American intrigues" having virtually wrecked the Franco-German alliance. He is firmly convinced that the United States, first under Kennedy and now under Johnson, has ruined his "masterpiece," a Franco-German reconciliation which he had hoped would permit France to become the leader of that partnership and to regain in that way the status of a world power. "Such an alliance," I was told, "could have been of some concern to the Russians and perhaps to others in Eastern Europe or even to Britain. But the Americans should have welcomed the prospect of one big power emerging in Western Europe which could once and for all bar the progress of communism on the continent, thus freeing the United States from a burden she has not been able to get rid of for two decades."

Then of course there is the war in Vietnam. To de Gaulle, the deepening American commitment is immensely serious, because sooner or later all of America's allies (and he always considers France as an American ally) may become involved, no matter how much they resist it. One of the reasons Washington has ignored de Gaulle's warnings against an overcommitment in Vietnam, so the general reasons, is that the United States has assumed that all other world problems can for the moment be put to one side. "Other problems" include America's relations with France and the American role in Western Europe. By demanding a radical transformation of NATO, de Gaulle hopes to show Mr. Johnson that Vietnam is far less crucial than the White House thinks.

Finally, one cannot understand French diplomacy today without taking into account de Gaulle's basic conviction that the United States is misusing its tremendous economic strength to establish American dominance throughout the world, under the pretext of a mission to halt communism. De Gaulle does not dismiss Communist dangers, but he considers that Washington is not ordained to intervene everywhere in the world; and that more often than not, when it does intervene, it does so ineptly and for reasons that have little to do with the fight against communism.

Although Paris and Washington, indeed Paris and all the other Western capitals, now seem on a collision course, there is an evident desire in Paris not to overly dramatize the conflict: "Why get nervous about the possible disruption of NATO," I have been asked here, "if that body is moribund anyway?" NATO, in this view, is obsolete. It was created seventeen years ago when it seemed as if Stalin might any morning order his divisions westward, but where is the responsible leader in Western Europe today who fears a Soviet attack? De Gaulle is aware, of course, that twenty-five Soviet divisions are still stationed in Eastern Germany. But he thinks that were a new Stalin to emerge, determined on new military adventures, NATO forces— using only conventional weapons—would be badly beaten in Central Europe. The Soviets can always muster forces far more powerful than those available to the West. De Gaulle therefore concludes that the only effective reply to possible Soviet aggression is immediate atomic reprisal, not the "graduated response" to which Secretary McNamara is devoted. In place of NATO, de Gaulle prefers the more traditional military alliance—perhaps an American, British and French alliance—which, in the event of Soviet aggression in Europe, would be prepared to launch an atomic attack on Russian towns and production centers. It is this notion that seems to have been rejected by President Johnson in his reply last month to de Gaulle: "Reliance in crisis on independent action by separate forces in accordance with national plans, only loosely coordinated with joint forces and plans, seems to be dangerous for all concerned." De Gaulle is convinced that the type of alliance he has in mind would be such a powerful deterrent as to assure that it would never have to become operational. It is for this reason that de Gaulle and his advisers refuse to believe that the partial or even complete dismantling of NATO is of great moment; rather, they say, such a move would contribute to the opening of more promising negotiations between France and other countries.

As to the scope of such talks, they would be aimed at establishing nothing less than a new base for partnership between Western Europe and the United States, replacing the one which came into being as the consequence of the enormous American contribution to Hitler's defeat and the blocking of Stalin, and as a consequence of American wealth and postwar Europe's poverty.

NOW THAT FRANCE IS OUT OF NATO [5]

Allied defenses in Western Europe are undergoing their most drastic shakeup since the end of World War II.

France's departure from the North Atlantic Treaty Organization on July 1, by decree of President Charles de Gaulle, brought only slight physical changes in the command structure and deployment of forces. But, from now on, NATO never will be the same.

The shift out of France of an elaborate network of American military installations and 26,000 United States military personnel is under way, although it won't be completed for a year.

A German takes over. Most of the 2,400 French officers and men assigned to Supreme Headquarters, Allied Powers in Europe, outside Paris, and to command headquarters for Central Europe, at Fontainebleau, already have been withdrawn. The French commander of Allied forces in Central Europe has been replaced by a West German officer.

Preparations have begun for moving NATO headquarters out of France—probably to Belgium.

U.S. planes leaving. In the American pullout, two squadrons of C-130 transport aircraft—thirty-two planes—are being moved from the big base at Evreux, France, to a base at Mildenhall, in Britain. Six American reconnaissance squadrons stationed at three other bases in France are to start leaving within the next few weeks—some going to West Germany and others possibly to Italy and Spain, or back to the United States.

Fifteen of sixty French jet fighter aircraft in West Germany already have been recalled to France. The other planes, along with two antiaircraft-missile squadrons, 11,000 air force personnel and 60,000 army troops, are remaining for the present, although no agreement has been reached whether they will remain permanently and, if so, on what terms.

[5] From article in *U.S. News & World Report*. 61:46+. Jl. 18, '66. Reprinted from *U.S. News & World Report*, published at Washington.

The United States informed France that, from July 1, nuclear bombs and warheads no longer would be available for these air and ground units in West Germany. These weapons have been stockpiled at or near French bases in Germany, but under American custody. The arrangement was that, in an emergency, they would be released to the French. But this agreement now has lapsed.

Not so bad, after all. All these changes—and others to come— are creating understandable confusion, but the result gives no indication of becoming the complete disaster that some Western officials first feared.

In the nuclear age, NATO strategists say, the theory that positions on French territory are indispensable to Europe's defense is no longer valid.

For more than ten years, the idea of a protracted defense, with large-scale ground fighting in the World War II pattern, in the event of a Russian attack, has been ruled out.

Rather, NATO strategy now is based on the use of nuclear weapons as soon as it should become clear that the Russians were engaged in a deliberate assault against Western Europe and not just in a probing operation or an accidental encounter.

United States Defense Secretary Robert S. McNamara told a Senate committee recently:

Neither the United States nor its allies have ever contemplated a war in which falling back on French soil through the battlefield of Germany was an acceptable strategy for the alliance.

Our military strategy is and remains the forward defense of Western Europe, which means, in Central Europe, a defense at the frontier of Western Germany. Our commitments, our deployments, our stategy and our forces are oriented as far as possible to that forward strategy, and to the use of whatever force and weapons may be necessary to achieve this forward defense.

In these plans, NATO sources concede, French participation and territory are highly valuable for headquarters sites, the most convenient supply and communications lines and supply dumps, as well as dispersal bases for aircraft. But the strategic plans, the experts say, will be affected only marginally by the withdrawal of France from NATO. The biggest, toughest task caused by the French action is the need to move sixteen huge American supply dumps and other installations. Until recently, United States policy has been to try to build stockpiles sufficient to maintain six American divisions in West Germany, as well as reinforcements, for ninety days of combat. Although this level has not been attained, the stocks of every imaginable type of military equipment that have accumulated in France are immense.

Some of these stockpiles are to be moved to new depots in West Germany, but at reduced levels. The United States intention now is to maintain supplies and equipment capable of supporting American forces in Europe for thirty-five to forty-five days in combat, rather than ninety days.

The shift of this matériel to West Germany is expected to take well over a year. The French have indicated they would have no objection if the moving job ran to the end of 1967.

For more than a year, the United States has been developing an alternative to the supply lines through France in anticipation of a French breakaway from NATO. Bremerhaven, in West Germany, has replaced La Rochelle, in France, as the main port of entry for supplies for American forces in Germany.

It's still uncertain whether the United States will be forced to seek access to pipelines through the Low Countries to deliver gasoline and oil to its forces in Germany. High-ranking officials hope now that the 550-mile pipeline built by NATO through France will be available in the future on a commercial basis.

If this proves feasible, these officials say, it still would be necessary to have access to standby pipeline facilities in the Low Countries for use in an emergency should France, for political reasons, choose to close its pipeline.

Who's going to pay? The massive shift of NATO and American military installations out of France is to cost a minimum of 500 million—and possibly as much as 1 billion—dollars. American officials say that France has a technical financial liability, but no one expects any money to be forthcoming from Paris to meet the costs.

The fourteen remaining NATO allies will have to foot the bill on a prorata basis, with the United States expected to contribute roughly 25 per cent.

The question of flights by allied military aircraft over France in the future is a crucial outstanding issue between President de Gaulle and NATO. At present, allied aircraft are permitted to overfly France under an agreement that is renewable monthly. Whether the French will agree to continue this arrangement in the future is uncertain.

A French ban on such overflights, officials say, would create serious difficulties for the United States and other NATO allies, which would face a "neutral air barrier" of France, Switzerland and Austria. This would all but cut NATO in two—separating the headquarters in Belgium and allied forces in Central Europe from direct air contact with the countries of the southern flank, Italy, Greece and Turkey.

Plans are being drafted to redeploy the so-called "ace" mobile force, a "fire-fighting" unit to deal quickly with any crisis that might develop on NATO's northern or southern flanks. Part of this force, it's said, probably would be based in Italy, or one of the other southern-flank countries, to avoid any overflight difficulties with France in the event of an emergency.

Prospects of a deal. A deal between France and NATO that would include continuing overflight privileges is being explored. These proposals are linked to plans for construction of a $300 million NATO system of early warning and communications that would provide information on air activity far behind the Iron Curtain and coordinate instantaneously the response of all Western defense weapons.

The French have indicated that they would contribute 12 per cent of the cost of such a system, even though they are now out of NATO. Without this and other NATO early-warning systems, it's pointed out, the French atomic defenses would be totally blind.

One big, outstanding question is this: What link, if any, do the French intend to maintain with NATO in the form of liaison officers, preparing contingency plans for coordinated action in an emergency and joint maneuvers?

De Gaulle has made it clear that he will accept no arrangement that would commit French forces automatically to come under the integrated NATO command at a specified stage of an emergency, or commit France automatically to respond. De Gaulle, who insists France remains loyal to the Atlantic alliance, says that he will go to the aid of the allies only in case of "unprovoked" aggression.

Negotiations now under way may produce the answer to the question of what ties, if any, France intends to maintain with NATO. These talks involve the status and role of French forces in West Germany. The French would like to leave these units in Germany, more or less with the status of occupation forces.

A silver lining. All in all, most NATO officials are confident that they can cope with the strictly military problems of a NATO without France and that NATO can survive as an effective deterrent to Soviet aggression in Europe.

One veteran observer in Paris says:

"There is certainly a silver lining to all this. With the French out, we can move ahead in lots of planning areas where the French had been obstructive.

"Because the French didn't like them, we had to 'talk around' such subjects as flexible response and force planning. Now, perhaps we can tackle these questions and make some progress."

Copyright 1966 U.S. News & World Report, Inc.

NATO WITHOUT FRANCE: THE IMPACT [6]

In a press conference held in late 1965, de Gaulle warned his allies that France would, by 1969 at the latest, end "the subordination known as 'integration' which is provided for by NATO and which hands our fate over to foreign authority."

De Gaulle's warning was turned into a program of action more quickly than his allies anticipated. In 1966 the French

[6] From *Great Decisions 1967*. (Fact Sheet no 7. NATO in Crisis—Will the Atlantic Alliance Survive?) Foreign Policy Association. 345 E. 46th St. New York 10017. '67. p 74-6. Copyright 1967 by the Foreign Policy Association, Inc. Reprinted by permission.

president carried out his break with NATO by ending French participation in its military command structure and ordering the removal of almost all foreign military forces from French soil by April 1967.

Severing the Ties

Under NATO accords, the allies, largely with United States financial support, had built a costly network of installations (bases, depots, airfields, communications facilities and pipelines) on French territory. In announcing his intention to take France out of the military alliance, de Gaulle declared that all NATO commands and installations in France would be required to come under French control or leave French soil. Rather than place NATO forces under French command—a step which repudiates the principle of integration—the allies are abandoning their installations and removing their forces, principally some 26,000 United States troops, from France.

The United States has already withdrawn six air squadrons; it is closing all of its bases and transferring communications facilities and supply depots to neighboring NATO countries. It may also have to relocate the oil pipeline that runs across France and into West Germany. Supplies for United States forces in Europe, which once flowed across France through the Atlantic ports of Bordeaux and La Rochelle, are now being routed through North Sea ports.

Most of the remaining ties between France and the NATO command are in the process of being severed. France has withdrawn its representatives from the Military Committee, NATO's senior military body, and from the now discarded Standing Group, the former executive agency of the Military Committee. NATO aircraft must receive monthly permission to fly over French territory. And France has ceased making financial contributions to the organization's military expenses, except for a few activities in which it chooses to participate, such as the air defense warning system. French forces and bases will be available to NATO in the event of an "unprovoked aggression," though France alone will decide when such an aggression occurs.

A number of other problems have arisen in the wake of the French withdrawal. One of these concerns the amount of money France will pay for the complex of installations left behind by the United States and other NATO members. A more important issue involves the status of the two French divisions stationed in West Germany and hitherto committed to NATO. Bonn wanted these forces to stay on as a symbol of continued French commitment to West Germany's defense. France agreed to this but insisted that the two divisions be detached from the NATO framework. Future cooperation between these French forces and NATO forces in Germany, the French argued, should be settled at the military level in direct negotiations between the French and allied commanders. The allies, for their part, pressed the French to settle these problems within the NATO council. When the French made it clear they would refuse to discuss the matter within that forum, however, the allies yielded. Last October [1966] they agreed that the future role of French forces in West Germany should be settled in a bilateral accord with Bonn and in direct negotiations between the Supreme Allied Commander in Europe, General Lyman L. Lemnitzer, and the French chief of staff, General Charles Ailleret.

The Organizational Impact

The French departure is causing a number of other changes in NATO's military structure. Until France withdrew, the Standing Group was composed of high-ranking military representatives of Britain, France and the United States, together with a West German observer. After the Standing Group was abandoned, the Military Committee, with its integrated planning staff, assumed the function of providing over-all strategic guidance for NATO forces.

Other organizational revisions will be required. The strategic area covered by the North Atlantic Treaty is divided into a Canada-United States Regional Planning Group and three separate commands: the Channel Command, the Atlantic Ocean

Command and the European Command. The latter, the most important of all, is under the authority of General Lemnitzer, whose headquarters, known as SHAPE (Supreme Headquarters Allied Powers, Europe), has been located on French soil outside Paris. French officers hitherto serving in these commands have been detached, and SHAPE itself is being moved to Belgium. Other integrated subcommands in France are also being moved— to England, the Netherlands, Germany and Italy—and new staff will be required to fill the French vacancies.

Despite these dislocations, the North Atlantic Council—the highest political body of the alliance—carries on with French participation. The council, on which each NATO member is represented, usually serves as a meeting ground for governmental ministers two or three times a year. Permanent representatives meet weekly, or more often if required, thereby ensuring the body's continuous functioning.

The council is the only formal organ mentioned in the North Atlantic Treaty, which describes its function vaguely as that of considering "matters concerning the implementation of this treaty." . . . In practice, as NATO has evolved, the council has concerned itself with over-all coordination of alliance policy on major political questions and on military matters that have significant political implications—for example, the establishment of military force levels for NATO defense. The council also ratifies basic defense strategy as negotiated in the Military Committee and approved by the defense ministers of each member. Most importantly of all, the council serves as the organ for consultation when aggression is threatened or committed—consultation in which France will continue to participate.

In recent meetings of the council, the French have continued to sit in as observers while matters of a strictly military nature were being discussed. Generally speaking, a "committee of 14" (all members except France) is now making those decisions from which France has chosen to dissociate itself. In order to maintain close liaison with NATO's military command, the council is also moving its headquarters from Paris to Belgium. . . .

What Integration Means

The creation of an integrated NATO military structure did not get under way until the Korean war alerted the allies to their own inadequate preparation for coping with a conventional attack in Europe. Thus, in point of time, the establishment of an integrated command structure followed rather than coincided with the formation of NATO. It was deemed necessary not only to insure greater readiness and coordination in case of war but for reasons of economy and efficiency as well. Such factors as weapons standardization and a commonly maintained infrastructure of supplies, communications, etc. were considered necessary to reduce the costly duplications involved in the maintenance of separate defense establishments.

What has integration meant in practice? In concrete terms it has meant primarily that the various NATO commands, such as SHAPE, have been staffed on an international basis for purposes of training, planning and coordination. It has also meant that the rearmament of West Germany could go forward within the NATO framework. (West Germany is the only NATO member whose troops are all formally committed to the NATO command; the Bundeswehr has no general staff of its own.) It has meant joint exercises held under NATO auspices and directed by NATO commands. And it has meant direct NATO control over a limited number of "quick reaction" fighters based on forward airfields in West Germany—fighters supplied by the United States, Canada, West Germany and, previously, France.

Integration has *not* meant supranational control of allied armies in time of peace, however. All combat forces earmarked for NATO defense remain under sovereign national command. They can be withdrawn, enlarged or eliminated at national will. Even the West German forces cannot be used without Bonn's assent. In the event of war, of course, NATO possesses the machinery to begin exercising immediate integrated command over all national forces assigned to it. But even this wartime command function cannot be assumed until each government has given the order transferring its national forces to NATO control.

Thus the more than 200,000 United States troops in Germany, which make up the most powerful element of the alliance's conventional strength, are assigned to NATO defense, but are under the control of the United States as long as peace prevails. Similarly, the United States strategic nuclear arsenal, located in the United States, in Polaris-missile submarines and in the overseas bases of the Strategic Air Command, is exclusively controlled by the United States President. The allies cannot trigger it into action unless the President gives the word; nor can they prevent it from being used in crises which they feel do not vitally concern them. As for the tactical nuclear weapons supplied by the United States to its NATO allies: these are controlled by a "double key" system which prevents their being fired without the permission of both the United States and the government of the country in which they are located.

Integration, therefore, has not meant that each member of NATO has had its hands tied by a supranational authority. Nor has it prevented some NATO members from using their armed forces as they saw fit, in behalf of their own national interests. The French, for example, withdrew some of their NATO troops from West Germany to fight in Algeria. The United States has withdrawn some of its troops for service in Vietnam. Though NATO planners can *advise* member states on troop levels, weapons development, etc., they cannot *enforce* compliance with their recommendations. And, in fact, recommended troop levels in Europe have never been fully attained.

The Strategic Impact

How seriously will the French departure from NATO affect its ability to safeguard Western Europe from aggression? The answer is disputed. Some observers, minimizing the importance of NATO's integrated command structure, contend that as long as France continues to adhere to the North Atlantic Treaty its withdrawal from the integrated command need not endanger Western defenses. Indeed, there is nothing to prevent France and NATO from negotiating new accords for joint action in the event of war.

United States officials, and those in most other NATO nations, view the consequences of the French withdrawal differently, however. The integration principle, they argue, is necessary in time of peace, for it is then that the allies must prepare for the eventuality of war. The delicate balance of forces that serves to deter war in Europe requires virtually instant readiness on the part of Allied forces—the ability to plan for and respond to a wide variety of provocations.

Various strategic problems have arisen in the wake of the French action. According to some military strategists, NATO cannot conduct a nonnuclear defense of Europe without French territory to fall back on. The critical area across West Germany is less than 100 miles wide at some points—allowing little room for maneuver or a "conventional pause" in the event of a Soviet attack. Yet such a pause is considered essential to the United States strategy of "flexible response." That strategy provides for meeting a Soviet thrust with conventional arms in the hope of obtaining time during which an escalation to nuclear conflict could be avoided and peace restored.

The doctrine of flexible response, though never formally endorsed by NATO, has been advocated by the United States as a replacement for NATO's older and formal doctrine of "massive retaliation," which presupposes an all-out nuclear reply to any Soviet attack. The French, however, have consistently rejected the theory of flexible response and have clung to massive retaliation as the best deterrent strategy to cope with any aggressive move from the East.

By quitting the NATO command structure, France has, in the view of some observers, made it more difficult for NATO to follow a strategy of flexible response and thus may have made it more likely that, if war breaks out, the strategy of massive retaliation will be the only response open to the West.

The Deeper Consequences

In the last analysis the consequences of the French withdrawal go deeper than matters of strategy or logistics. They involve intangible—but even more important—factors of psychology, morale and purpose. The enthusiasm and hopes which NATO generated in the early years of the cold war have diminished. Its indispensability is being questioned. The French withdrawal, moreover, comes at a time when the alliance is undergoing other difficulties. Britain and the United States are currently involved in a dispute with the Bonn government over how much the latter should pay to offset the foreign-exchange costs of the British and American forces stationed in West Germany. A reappraisal of the issue is under way. But if Bonn refuses to pay as much as the United States and Britain consider necessary, the result could be a cutback in United States and British troops.

DE GAULLE'S EUROPE [7]

If the principal motive of the European idea today is the desire for autonomy and status, it is not surprising that the Gaullist idea of "Europe" has a considerable appeal to Europeans, despite the fact that de Gaulle is so adamantly opposed to the supranationalism which, to the classical "Europeans," is the hallmark of the European idea.

United States power and Europe's military dependence give Europeans the feeling that they do not control their own political destiny. For citizens of former great powers, this is a source of serious and growing frustration.

President de Gaulle's design for Europe has attracted Europeans because it expresses the feelings and hopes which they are less free than he to make explicit. Germans are still too concerned about security to follow de Gaulle wholeheartedly, even if his ambiguous policy toward Eastern Europe were less worrisome to them than it is. The British, with their sense of historical affinity to the United States and their doubts about both France and Germany, are still less able to be Gaullists. Yet in both countries and elsewhere in Western Europe there is a great

[7] From *Atlantic Alliance: Problems and Prospects*, pamphlet by H. van B. and J. B. Cleveland, economists and political analysts. (Headline Series no 177) Foreign Policy Association. 345 E. 46th St. New York 10017. Je. '66. p 45-7. Copyright 1966 by the Foreign Policy Association, Inc. Reprinted by permission.

deal of more or less ambivalent admiration for this harsh, authoritarian, but strangely impressive, "David," who so impudently challenges the American "Goliath" and who seems to promise not only the withdrawal from Europe of United States power, but of Soviet power as well.

For these reasons, Gaullism, insofar as it is the expression of Europeans' desire to be masters of their own destiny, is likely to survive its author as a continuing political force in Europe. But the Gaullist design of a "European Europe" based on a Western European coalition under French leadership is essentially unrealistic, because France does not possess the material power and the prestige which such leadership would require.

For de Gaulle, European independence is the end and European unity the means. Until a European majority comes to share his view, a supranational union would not serve the purpose of independence. On the contrary, it would have the opposite effect. It would submerge France in a European majority which accepts the United States protectorate. President de Gaulle seems to believe that without a strong common will to independence, no effective European government could arise. Until Europe has that will, a "Europe of states" is preferable to a Europe united enough to restrict national freedom of action, but not enough to do without United States protection.

De Gaulle's design requires a Germany willing to accept French leadership. When de Gaulle came to power, the psychological basis for such a relationship existed and may still exist today. Germany is still quite passive in its foreign relations, due to its sense of military insecurity and fear of disturbing its neighbors. Moreover, most Germans regard with profound satisfaction the Franco-German reconciliation. Psychology, however, is not enough. For his design to succeed, de Gaulle must offer Germans tangible benefits in return for political dependence: in particular, military protection against Soviet power. He must also be able to reassure Germany's neighbors (Frenchmen included) of his ability to restrain a potentially nationalistic Germany.

These things he plainly lacks the power to do. In consequence, he has felt it necessary to seek closer ties with Eastern Europe and the Soviet Union as a means of increasing his political leverage on Germany. In so doing he defeats his own objective by undermining German trust in France.

On the one hand, he toasts [former] Chancellor Ludwig Erhard with eloquent words about the European union which France and Germany are building together. On the other hand, he courts Eastern Europe and begins an ambiguous flirtation with the Soviet Union as though to say to Germany, "I have other ways of controlling you if you should refuse my leadership."

Such a policy is the product and evidence of weakness. It is an attempt by a relatively weak power to accomplish by maneuver what the United States is able to do directly by offering Germany a mutually beneficial bargain, in which United States protection is exchanged for German acceptance of United States leadership. In the end, in the authors' opinion, de Gaulle's German policy must be self-defeating. Either it will tend to strengthen German dependence on the United States; or it will drive Germans to look out for their own security and their Eastern interests by a more independent and active foreign policy of their own.

De Gaulle's design would substitute France for the United States as Western Europe's leader. But the United States capacity to lead Europe is the product of qualifications, material and political, which are not easy to match. In a coalition whose functional purpose is military security, effective leadership presupposes not only the military power to protect Europe but the prestige which past military success and reliability as an ally have created. In a coalition whose ideological purpose is to protect democratic institutions, leadership presupposes the prestige of success in this sphere as well. French democracy lacks prestige even in France; de Gaulle has never concealed his contempt for traditional French parliamentary democracy. The American image may be a bit tarnished, but there is no substitute to be found on the other side of the Atlantic.

WHO IS THE REAL REALIST? [8]

At the top of Brussels' Rue de la Loi where a sixteenth-century monastery once stood, hundreds of workers are putting the finishing touches on a massive thirteen-story octagon designed to serve as the new headquarters of the European Common Market. By the time "La Maison de l'Europe" is completed next year, the Belgians will have spent close to $50 million on what they hope will become Europe's first "Federal District." "De Gaulle permitting, that is," grumbles the chief foreman on the job.

The foreman's worry is legitimate. France has been boycotting all meetings of the European Common Market since June 30. [France has since ended its boycott—Ed.] The trouble started last spring [1965] when the Common Market Executive, headed by Germany's Professor Walter Hallstein, rather imprudently overreached its mandate and tried to turn the Six's common agricultural fund into an embryonic federal budget.

In the first days after the French walkout, the other five members of the Common Market talked boldly of completing the European edifice themselves—on the assumption that one day France would return. Meanwhile, they said, Britain would take France's place. But Britain gave no sign of wishing to play the game without France. Just the contrary: "The idea of building Europe around an isolated France is not practicable," editorialized the London *Times*.

The only way out, the five eventually concluded, was to get France back. But on what terms?

Conditions: De Gaulle's conditions boil down to this: the Common Market must not develop into anything more than a customs union (which is all it is now, and only two-thirds completed at that). Further, the European Community must be drained of all supranational content. Then the Common Market could join in a loose confederation with its rival, the seven-nation European Free Trade Association, led by Britain.

[8] From article by Arnaud de Borchgrave, European correspondent. *Newsweek*. 66: 45-7. D. 13, '65. Copyright, Newsweek, Inc., December, 1965. Reprinted by permission.

Outraged by these proposals, de Gaulle's foes make it sound as though the general is alone in opposing the federal European state that the men who launched the Common Market intended it to become. Actually, however, all of the Market's member nations are today less disposed to make meaningful sacrifices of national sovereignty than they were when Europe was still recovering from World War II. Then, almost all Europeans unquestioningly accepted the slogan "Integrate or Perish."

But Europe did not integrate—and it did not perish. In fact, Europe has never been more prosperous. But myths die hard. And the theologians of federalism in Brussels (and Washington) have dug their heels in. We Six, goes their implicit credo, have a preordained right to call ourselves Europe because we established the Common Market with the Treaty of Rome. Other nations have the choice of signing that treaty—or of staying out of "Europe."

But unless a federal state of Europe can be created in the foreseeable future—and clearly it cannot—there is little point in continuing economic integration with only six states. As an alternative, France's Louis Armand, former president of Euratom, suggests what has become known as "Federalism à la carte." Under his plan, there would be no single European Community but a number of European communities. Thus, ten nations might decide they could unite in the field of transportation, five on the reciprocity of law degrees and perhaps as many as twenty-five on a common patent law. Even some Eastern European countries might decide they could join a merger effort in clearly defined, nonpolitical areas.

Instant federalism: Should something of this kind ultimately occur, it may well prove that, by forcing Europeans to face up to the impracticality of instant federalism, de Gaulle has actually contributed significantly to the final realization of a broader European unity. Similarly, what the United States regards as the general's obstreperous refusal to cooperate with NATO may eventually produce a new and more realistic approach to Europe's military-diplomatic problems.

For years, it has been Washington dogma that integration of West Germany into NATO and a European federal state would lead to reunification of the two Germanies. The theory was that as Moscow's control collapsed in Eastern Europe, NATO's frontiers would be pushed to the Soviet border and East Germany would be freed to rejoin West Germany on the West's terms.

Cold-war attitudes: By this logic, integration with the West both militarily and politically had to be the keystone of Bonn's foreign policy. West German Chancellor Ludwig Erhard [since replaced] and Foreign Minister Gerhard Schroeder, in fact, are both still prisoners of such cold-war attitudes—as is evidenced by their demand for nuclear equality for West Germany within the Western alliance.

Yet it has now become utterly apparent that Russia both can and will maintain East Germany indefinitely as a separate state so long as West Germany is militarily tied to the United States. As a result, a growing number of Germans are beginning to believe that integration precludes rather than facilitates, the reunification process. . . .

United States policymakers believe that it was Gaullism that sparked the new wave of German nationalism, but many European experts will tell you that the wave was about to break no matter what. And quite apart from the pressures from within Germany, relations between the Soviet bloc and the West have now reached a point where the next important advances will depend upon some kind of settlement in Central Europe. This is de Gaulle's conviction and the departure point of his policy. Erhard, however, believes just the opposite. And that, briefly, is why Bonn and Paris are now at dagger's point.

It was only three years ago that de Gaulle signed France's historic treaty of eternal friendship with West Germany. He hoped to use that treaty to force Germany's leaders to "think European" rather than go on lulling themselves to sleep in the Atlantic crib. But the attempt failed, and de Gaulle has only himself to blame. Had it not been for his virulent anti-Americanism, which even many Gaullists find objectionable and which utterly alienated Bonn, Europe would probably by now have found the "distinct" personality and policy that he seeks to give it.

Not only did Bonn's leaders turn down de Gaulle, they concluded in 1964 a momentous, though little publicized, military agreement with the United States. In effect, as de Gaulle sees it, Germany agreed under the pact to remain a United States client state for the next decade. The general had vetoed Britain's bid to enter the Common Market for less and now West Germany was replacing Britain as the American Trojan horse in Europe.

Entente: Faced with this, de Gaulle sought to use Russia as a counterweight. As long as the Paris-Bonn axis had existed, Moscow was not interested in de Gaulle's overtures. But the moment that axis broke, a Franco-Soviet entente flourished. And now de Gaulle has suddenly decided that Britain, too, has become acceptable again. London, as well as Moscow, is needed to counterbalance what one recent visitor heard the general refer to as "the threat of an American-German condominium in Europe."

Nothing has been helped by recent Washington talk of arming Germany with intermediate-range ballistic missiles that would bring Russia within reach of German striking power for the first time since World War II. This seems calculated to upset the Russians even more than the establishment of twelve West German conventional divisions has already done. Some Europeans openly wonder whether the Pentagon and Bonn are not in league to torpedo the chances of a Central European settlement as well as a nuclear nonproliferation treaty.

Whatever the intention, that would be the almost certain consequence of giving the Germans partial control of nuclear weapons. De Gaulle, meantime, is trying to show Bonn that the solution to the European problem lies in a different direction. In essence, his point is that military integration of NATO makes no sense without a common political purpose. And what should that purpose be, now that the Soviet military threat to Europe has largely dissipated and German reunification on purely Western terms has become a chimera?

In the face of this, Washington continues to argue that more integration, not less, is what is needed to get NATO out of its present doldrums. Pooh-poohing suggestions that what has shielded Europe from Russian conquest has been the United States nuclear arsenal rather than NATO integration, United States policymakers now declare that if de Gaulle will not go along with even more integration, the alliance should be reorganized without France. . . .

Much of the trouble between Paris and Washington, of course, stems from the fact that de Gaulle has not done much to help the United States understand what he is about and what he is trying to achieve. He attacks NATO as an instrument of American hegemony, tries to subvert the dollar and takes a variety of other actions that make him seem more enemy than friend. Yet, there are encouraging new signs that his style toward the United States is changing. One is that Charles E. Lucet, the . . . French ambassador to Washington, has been instructed by the general to begin a quiet, dispassionate dialogue with the United States.

Europe-wide community: If Lucet succeeds in doing so, United States policymakers might be brought to see that de Gaulle is advocating no more than some of their own advisers do. As a result of some studies of European affairs he has made for LBJ during the past year, Professor Zbigniew Brzezinski, Columbia University political scientist, has concluded that a Europe-wide cooperative community with "America and Russia as the peripheral participants, and West and East Europe as the two halves of the inner core . . . would provide a more constructive and politically appealing image of tomorrow than a troubled Western partnership based on the notion of continued European partition."

In the final analysis, there is no real crisis in the West. Lives are not at stake. The difficulties of NATO and the Common Market merely reflect a deep-seated malaise. To decide to go stubbornly ahead with either institution without France begs the real issue. Solutions are not easy, but ultimately they must lie in slicing through the fog of clichés that currently blankets the Atlantic world and recognizing the necessity for an end to the present artificial divisions of the old Continent.

DE GAULLE'S EUROPEAN STRATEGY [9]

In 1944, General de Gaulle saw his future looming. He says in his memoirs that he already had a plan to unite the fragments of Europe in "an organized association of peoples from Iceland to Istanbul and from Gibraltar to the Urals." But to achieve this, the Soviets first had to be kept out of the heart of Europe. It was "essential" that the independence of the countries of Eastern Europe and the Balkans be protected from acquisitive "bolshevism."

De Gaulle spoke of this to Churchill when the two men met in Paris on November 13, 1944. He proposed that France and Britain work together to form "an organization of peoples which would be something other than a field for the quarrels of America and Russia." But Churchill did not think the Soviets could be stopped. De Gaulle quotes him as saying: "Russia is a big beast who has been hungry for a very long time. It is impossible to prevent her from eating, especially since she has reached the very middle of the flock of victims."

Three months later, Churchill went to Yalta with Roosevelt. De Gaulle, uninvited, stayed at home. In a broadcast the day after the Crimea conference opened, he said France would not be bound by any agreement that did not safeguard the independence of the East. This was one of the "essential conditions" for peace in Europe, he said. The rest is history. Yalta cut Europe in two. The cold war set one half against the other. The nuclear monopoly tied each half to the policies of its protector. The cradle of Western civilization became the subdivided backyard of the superpowers.

This fate may have been inevitable, but de Gaulle has never accepted it as immutable. In fact, he predicted the desatellization of Eastern Europe before the process of satellization was even complete. Six months after Yalta, in an August 1945 meeting in Washington with Truman, he said: "With the consent of America and Great Britain, the states of Central and Balkan Europe are forced to serve as satellites of the Soviet Union." For the moment,

[9] From article by James Edwards, Paris correspondent for Radio Free Europe. *East Europe.* 15:2-8. N. '66. Reprinted by permission.

they were tied by "bonds of force," but this was a situation that would not last forever. If the fear of German revival could be removed, then the "national interests" of the satellites would not fail to arise. The Soviets themselves would eventually lose their taste for "adventure," and unrest within their empire would further divert them from warlike undertakings."

But that was the future. This was 1945 and Europe's division was a fact. De Gaulle faced up to it. In a speech at Brussels University on October 11 of that year, he still spoke of "the hope that, one day, could be given to the whole world by the association of all the peoples of Europe," but he proposed for the near future "a Western grouping having as its arteries the Rhine, the Channel and the Mediterranean." Greater Europe was deferred; it was not abandoned. Of course, de Gaulle did not stay to see his "interim" solution of West European unity enacted. He resigned as premier of France in January 1946 and retired to Colombey-les-Deux-Églises to wait twelve years in the wilderness for his recall.

Return to Power

It was Algeria that brought the general back to office as premier in 1958, then as president in 1959, and it was naturally the war in North Africa, with its associated risk of civil war in the Metropole [i.e. France itself], that consumed his every waking hour during his first few months in office. But on November 10, 1959, in only his second press conference as president, he dealt with Europe at length. After the Khrushchev ultimatum on Berlin the previous year, the Soviets had simmered down and were being uncommonly restrained. De Gaulle offered five reasons for these signs of change. With an assurance that few Kremlinologists were showing seven years ago, he put his finger on five factors forcing evolution on the Soviet Union.

First, there was nuclear terror:

Having colossal power and knowing that the West has power of the same order, Russia undoubtedly admits that a conflict, from whatever side it may come, would lead to general annihilation and that one must turn from making war to making peace.

Second, the consumer pressures:

Without doubt, the Communist regime . . . is losing its virulence under the profound pressure of people towards what man by nature wants: a better life and liberty.

Third came the Chinese threat:

Soviet Russia, although it helped install communism in China, undoubtedly sees that, whatever it may do, it is still Russia—white nation of Europe, conqueror of a part of Asia and very well-endowed in land, mines, factories and riches—faced by the yellow horde that is China, innumerable and miserable, indestructible and ambitious, building . . . a power one cannot measure and looking around itself at the expanses into which it will one day have to spread itself.

Fourth, the uneasy empire of Eastern Europe:

This same regime, which Russia has used to govern by force, through intermediaries, the territories of its neighbors of Europe, doubtlessly recognizes that though it reigns over [the countries of Eastern Europe], it has not acquired them and that the populations, if they could express themselves freely, would reject that regime by an enormous majority.

Fifth and finally, de-Stalinization: "Perhaps above all," de Gaulle said, the decisive role in the beginning of "a new orientation" had been played by Nikita Khrushchev who realized that "at the supreme level of responsibility, service rendered to man, to his conditions, to his peace is the most realistic of realisms, the most politic of policies."

Six months after de Gaulle made that statement, U-2 pilot Francis Gary Powers took off for a routine flight. The signs of Soviet softening vanished overnight. But the U-2 incident and the freeze that followed in no way invalidated any one of de Gaulle's five factors. He continued to call attention to them, even when Soviet actions seemed to be running against the tide that he had charted.

One example among many was his press conference of September 5, 1960. The Paris Summit had collapsed. The Eastern countries had walked out of the disarmament conference in Geneva. Khrushchev himself was blasting the West at the United Nations in New York. But de Gaulle said:

Despite the constraint, isolation and acts of force with which the Communist regime shuts in the countries under its yoke . . . its gaps, its failings, its internal failures and, over and above all, its character of inhuman repression are felt more and more by the elites and the masses who are more and more difficult to bend and to delude. Also, the satellites that the Soviet regime holds under its law are finding the cruelty of their annexation more and more trying to their national sentiments.

This was his tone for several years: cutting condemnation of Communist repression combined with constant reminder of the evolutionary pressures and unflagging optimism in the eventual melting of the monolith.

The German Nettle

The year of change was 1963. The Algerian affair had been liquidated by the Évian accords of the previous year and the general was free to concentrate on Europe. His first move was to sign the Franco-German treaty of cooperation. The general had stressed in his 1945 meeting with Truman and later that Germany was the key to Greater Europe. The evolution of the eastern half of the continent could not progress beyond a certain point, so long as there was still a threat, real or imagined, of renewed German aggression. The basic national interest was survival and other, lesser interests could not assert themselves against Soviet primacy so long as Soviet strength was required to safeguard Eastern Europe against a German threat. By his treaty with Adenauer, de Gaulle hoped to put himself in a position to influence German evolution in a direction that would assuage East European concern. Also, since what de Gaulle was planning was a rapprochement of the two halves of his Greater Europe, he needed to carry Western Europe along with him in his campaign. Thus, the treaty with Bonn was opened to the accession of the other West Europeans. The theory was that they would rally to it, either positively, out of a desire to reinforce West European cooperation, or negatively, out of a desire to attenuate what looked like a bid to erect a Franco-German "axis" west of the Elbe.

But the general's tactic misfired. The Bundestag imposed a preamble that stripped the treaty of its special character. John F. Kennedy visited Germany in de Gaulle's footsteps and reasserted the special character of German-American relations. The multilateral nuclear force (MLF) project surfaced and its lure of a German nuclear role completed the process of erasing de Gaulle's initiative.

The Chinese Menace

Despite his setbacks, the general decided to go ahead with his "opening to the East." But before he did so, he made another move of special significance: in January 1964, France recognized Communist China. De Gaulle had placed an early emphasis on the significance of the Sino-Soviet rift and he had followed its development closely. By September 1963, he was satisfied that it had passed beyond the stage of a dispute "between tendencies and men" to become a "terrible opposition . . . between two great peoples." For de Gaulle, this was no doctrinal dispute, but a bitter clash of national interests that would be difficult if not impossible to resolve. When he sent his ambassador to Peking, he was recognizing China as a separate source of world power, independent of the Soviet Union. He was saying that a bi-polar pattern of power was evolving toward a triangular division of the world.

For Europe, the significance of this is inescapable. The continent today is divided between two superpowers. One is a land-mass straddling Europe and Asia. The other is a continent washed by the Atlantic and the Pacific. China, opposed to both, is an Asian *and* a Pacific power. It poses a threat both to the Pacific flank of the United States and to the Asian underbelly of the Soviet Union. De Gaulle believes that these facts must inevitably shift the scene of global confrontation from Europe to Asia. Already, Europe no longer has the undivided attention of its protectors. Furthermore, the Chinese distraction has arisen at a time when the cold war in Europe has been fought to a standstill, in brief, when peace is possible.

The general wants the Europeans to act now, to organize their own peace on the continent, while they still have this new room for maneuver. If they do not act, if they stay tied to protectors who now have vital interests beyond the European theater, then they run a double risk: they could become either the victims of a war that starts outside of Europe or the victims of a superpower settlement imposed on Europe with the aim of avoiding a two-front confrontation.

Turning Toward Eastern Europe

De Gaulle finally launched France on its rapprochement with Eastern Europe in July 1964, when he received Rumanian Premier Ion Gheorghe Maurer in Paris. The two countries lost no time building on this beginning. Within six months, there had been Paris visits by Rumanian Deputy Premier Alexandre Birladeanu, Foreign Minister Corneliu Manescu and a Rumanian parliamentary delegation. There had also been Bucharest visits by French Minister of Industry Michel Maurice-Bokanowski, Finance Minister Valéry Giscard d'Estaing and a French parliamentary delegation. In addition, a five-year Franco-Rumanian trade pact aiming at 100 per cent expansion of commerce was negotiated and signed in the same period.

In those same six months, Paris received visits from a Bulgarian deputy premier, the foreign ministers of Czechoslovakia, Hungary, Yugoslavia and Bulgaria, and the foreign trade minister of Poland. In the opposite direction, the French ministers of science and of information visited Moscow and the minister of industry went to Sofia.

Also in this initial burst of activity: a five-year trade pact with Moscow and two-year cultural accords with Prague and Sofia. That trade pact with Moscow has a significance of its own: it was signed barely two weeks after Khrushchev fell. Khrushchev had been one of de Gaulle's five factors favorable to evolution, yet when the Soviet leader so abruptly left the scene the general did not even break his step: while the world still wondered, France went through with the long-term accord and its incorporated promise of $350 million in credits. It was clear that de Gaulle was convinced that regardless of its author's fate, Khrushchevism was here to stay.

These first six months of the Gaullist "opening" brought the general very neatly to a date that must have been circled on his calendar: he scheduled his winter press conference of 1965 for February 4. On the twentieth anniversary of Yalta, he put forward his proposals for curing the condition that Yalta had created. Once again, he is worth quoting at length.

Germany's division, de Gaulle said, was the obstacle to "real peace" in Europe and the confrontation of two camps was the obstacle to a true solution of this problem:

What has to be done can only be done, one day, by the understanding and the united action of the peoples who have always been, who are and who will remain principally interested in the fate of the German neighbor: in brief, the European peoples.

These should envisage first examining together, then settling in common, and finally guaranteeing jointly the solution of a question which is essentially that of their continent.

That is the only way they can bring back and maintain in Europe a state of balance, peace and cooperation from one end to the other of the territory that nature has attributed to her.

Assuredly, the success of such a vast and difficult enterprise implies many conditions. It is necessary that Russia evolve in such a way that she sees her future no longer in totalitarian constraint imposed on her people and on others, but in progress accomplished together by free men and free peoples.

It is necessary that the nations she has made her satellites be able to play their role in a renewed Europe.

It is necessary that it be recognized . . . by Germany, that the solution of which she will be the object would necessarily imply the settlement of her frontiers and her armaments in agreement with all her neighbors, in the East and in the West. . . .

It is necessary that Europe, mother of modern civilization, establish herself from the Atlantic to the Urals in peace and cooperation. . . .

France, for her part, believes that [German question] cannot be resolved except by Europe herself. . . .

The great virtue of this approach, in the Gaullist view, is that it shifts the weight of the German problem. What was a road-block to rapprochement becomes a reward for rapprochement. Instead of saying: "Solve the German problem and then we can get together," de Gaulle said: "Let us get together and then we can solve the German problem." This aspect of his proposal was lost, however, in the wave of concern at the prospect that the United States was to be shut out of the general's Europe rebuilt by the Europeans.

The Russian Card

It may well have been this Pan-European flavor that brought the Soviets themselves rather abruptly into the field of French rapprochement, which until now had largely involved only the East Europeans. A bare six weeks after the general's press conference, Moscow named First Deputy Foreign Minister Valerian Zorin as new ambassador to Paris. This was no demotion of the number-two exponent of Soviet diplomacy, but it may have been the promotion of de Gaulle to number-one target of Soviet diplomacy.

The appointment removed Sergei Vinogradov, dean of the Paris diplomatic corps and an intimate of the general, but it installed, in Zorin, a former ambasador to Bonn and an expert on European affairs. And it put him in a position to have close and continuing contact with French Foreign Minister Maurice Couve de Murville, himself a former ambassador to Bonn.

Meanwhile, French contacts continued to multiply. In the six months following de Gaulle's press conference, there were Paris visits by Soviet Foreign Minister Andrei Gromyko, the education minister and a vice premier from Czechoslovakia and the foreign trade minister of Bulgaria. In the other direction, French Minister of State Louis Joxe went to Prague and French parliamentarians visited Prague, Warsaw and Bucharest. A five-year trade pact was negotiated with Poland and another was signed with Czechoslovakia.

This period brought de Gaulle to September 1965 and Poland's belated entry through his "eastern opening." Premier Jozef Cyrankiewicz came to Paris to round out a series of visits that had now reestablished relations with all East European countries, except Albania and, naturally, East Germany. De Gaulle scheduled a press conference for the day of the premier's arrival and publicly attached "great importance" to the new French policy of rapprochement. This press conference marked a new stage in de Gaulle's verbal "de-escalation" of the cold war.

During 1963, his optimism on the score of eventual East European evolution had grown more marked. During 1964, he had said that evolution away from old totalitarian methods was actually underway. Now, in September 1965, he dropped even such retroactive criticism. Relations had been normalized.

The six months following the Cyrankiewicz visit remained active. French "technical" ministers visited Warsaw, Budapest, Bucharest and Belgrade. There were long-term trade pacts with Hungary and Bulgaria, cultural accords with Rumania and Czechoslovakia and various scientific or technical cooperation agreements with Hungary, Poland, Rumania and Yugoslavia. It was in this period that Couve de Murville started repaying the Paris visits of his counterparts. He went to Moscow in October 1965. Among agreements he concluded there was one consolidating the earlier understanding for joint Franco-Soviet support of the French SECAM system for color television. A link-up of SECAM and the Soviet Molnya-I communications satellite beamed full-color films of flowers and fashions from Moscow to Paris.

By the end of 1965, France had set a new record for its trade exchanges with the Communist world: the $776 million two-way total was up 14 per cent over 1964, which had already shown an 11 per cent increase over 1963. As it marked this record, Paris enacted a sweeping liberalization of trade with the East. Quota restrictions were removed from close to 600 individual products. All Communist countries were covered by the reform, with the exception of East Germany, Cuba, North Korea and North Vietnam.

The liberalization was unilateral. No reciprocal concessions were sought from the countries of the East. Despite safeguard clauses, some sectors of French industry were concerned lest the reform open the door to dumping. The government was criticized for exacting no counterconcessions and the view was widespread that the plan had been pressed not by the economic ministries but by the Quai d'Orsay.

The current year has seen the completion of the bases for future French cooperation with the East. By the time the rapprochement policy had reached its second anniversary, long-term trade agreements had been signed with all the major countries of Eastern Europe: for six years with Yugoslavia, for five years with the Soviet Union, Poland, Czechoslovakia and Rumania, and for four years with Hungary and Bulgaria. The economic bases are built to last until 1970. At the same time, France has completed its exchange of high-level political visitors with all the European Communist countries, save Albania and again, of course, East Germany.

This process meant that in the period July 1964 to July 1966, literally no month was without its contribution to the policy of rapprochement. Every month without exception produced an agreement in one field or another or a ministerial visit in one direction or the other. In twenty-five months, France and the countries of the East exchanged some forty visits at ministerial level or higher. One president, two premiers, four deputy premiers and seven foreign ministers have been involved in this exchange. High-water mark so far in the rapprochement (perhaps pending the Kosygin visit to Paris or the much-awaited de Gaulle tour of Eastern Europe) has naturally been the general's own trip to Moscow last June.

Any attempt to draw a balance sheet of that visit runs into the problem of its relation to the earlier withdrawal from NATO. The most popular belief is that the NATO withdrawal was a preconcession from the French designed to elicit a counterconcession from the Soviets. French officials deny this. The Gaullist explanation of the NATO withdrawal is that it was a necessary move that, if it was to be made, was better made before rather than after the trip to Moscow. It was necessary for the reasons that such spokesmen as Premier Pompidou and Couve de Murville gave to the parliament and the press at the time: NATO's integrated system no longer guaranteed American nuclear intervention in a European war and now threatened Europe's implication in an American war starting in Asia and spreading to Europe. If the withdrawal also had a connection with the Moscow trip, the Gaullists say that connection lay in the fact that both actions were a declaration of French faith in the détente.

The fearful (or hopeful) expectations of dramatic developments from the general's visit sprang from an inadequate understanding of his aims and his approach. His aim, most definitely, is the eventual end of Germany's division which, for him, holds the seed of a new war in Europe. And his approach has been well established as "gradualist," at least since the Yalta-anniversary press conference.

De Gaulle did use Moscow to "sloganize" his approach. He outlined it in utter simplicity as *"détente, entente et coopération."* It is clear that the first stage is still in progress. Détente in Europe, so far, deeply affects only France. Eastern relations with other countries of the West still show lingering remnants of cold war attitudes. With none of them has the process of normalization reached the stage achieved by the French. And détente has to be secured before entente can materialize. So de Gaulle is fostering détente by example.

In a Kremlin toast on the first night of his visit, the general said that in seeking change in the international situation, France in talking to the East will "necessarily" address itself to Moscow. On the face of it, this may sound like a recognition of the very hegemony that the general has so frequently excoriated. But, in fact, de Gaulle has always recognized, since the 1945 talk with Truman, that the Soviets will maintain a grip as long as a German threat compels Eastern Europe to accept a self-defensive dependence on Moscow.

The German problem is the key that locks the East Europeans in. And that problem is made up of two parts, West Germany and East Germany. East Germany is directly controlled by the Soviets. So de Gaulle "necessarily" has to address himself to Moscow. But he also addresses himself to the East Europeans, and, since Moscow, he does so with Soviet sanction. In fact, of the series of sixteen bilateral discussions of the German problem that France has held with Eastern countries since July 1964, no fewer than twelve have been with East European leaders.

The Grand Design

The Grand Design will take a great leap forward on the day de Gaulle succeeds with the East Europeans in making the point, implicit in his entire approach, that the so-called German threat is not serious enough to justify the limitation it imposes on their freedom. On that day, the East Europeans will start to provide internal stimuli for a change in Moscow's attitude on East Germany and the German problem will start to crumble.

To do this, however, the general needs the help of Bonn. For Warsaw and Prague in particular, the West Germans are militarists and revanchists. It is not enough for France to say this is untrue, any more than it is for Bonn itself to issue such denials. The Germans have to show good faith: renounce all proximity to the nuclear trigger, whether in MLF or in any other similar project, and renounce the lost territories, through recognition now or a promise of later recognition of existing frontiers.

If de Gaulle can induce Bonn to emerge from what he does not hesitate to call its "immobilism" on these points, then progress toward a Europe stretching from the Atlantic to the Urals will become possible. And it is that Europe that will finally solve the German problem. The solution must be unification.

The other West Europeans remain to be convinced of either the desirablity or the feasibility of a Greater Europe embracing the Soviets. But there are increasing signs that they are now convinced of both the desirability and the possibility of a détente between the two existing postwar Europes. In the past few months, they have stated the case with growing optimism in such organizations as NATO, the Council of Europe and the Western European Union, and there has been a marked multiplication of official contacts. To cite just a few examples: Belgian Foreign Minister Pierre Harmel was recently in Warsaw, West Germany Secretary of State Rolf Lahr visited Sofia and Minister of Economics Kurt Schmueker visited Bucharest, Danish Foreign Minister Per Haekkerup was in Budapest, and British Foreign Secretary George Brown is due to visit Sofia and Bucharest.

Obviously, the other West Europeans have a long way to go before they can draw abreast of the advanced French position in Eastern Europe, built up by a concerted campaign of political and economic action that is now in its third year. But the trend is without doubt in the direction that de Gaulle first signaled when he received Rumanian Premier Maurer back in 1964. Whether the general can take any credit for the over-all trend may be debated. But the fact remains that Western Europe is accompanying France on the first step of de Gaulle's policy, that is, détente. The Gaullist hope is that as détente develops, entente will come to appear more practicable than it seems today and that the other West Europeans will one day find themselves embarked upon the second step as well.

Of course, the most certain thing about de Gaulle's Europe is that it will be built, if it is ever built, in the absence of the architect. The general enters his 77th year in November, and he is the first to insist that his is a plan *de longue haleine* [a long-range plan]. What he is doing now is breaking the ice and charting the course. He is offering what Sorbonne Professor Leo Harmon calls "an alternative to the Two Walls." Harmon says the Eastern policy up to now has been based on the concept of "the Great Wall of China" and it has been met by a Western policy based on the concept of "the Walls of Jericho." The East thought the wall of the iron curtain would be proof against the entry of any external element. The West thought the wall would come tumbling down in response to declamatory policies.

De Gaulle is ignoring the walls, ignoring the ideologies and setting up what he calls "secular relations" developing the détente. Meanwhile, in France's own unilateral dialogue with the East, he has ensured that the German problem stays open to discussion. Insoluble in today's atmosphere, it may slowly yield to progress in the new atmosphere of relaxation he is encouraging. If it yields, Europe's division will yield.

This, in any case, is his aim. Only history will say whether it will be his achievement.

BIBLIOGRAPHY

An asterisk (*) preceding a reference indicates that the article or a part of it has been reprinted in this book.

Books, Pamphlets, and Documents

Ambler, J. S. French army in politics: 1945-1962. Ohio State University Press. Columbus. '66.

Aron, Raymond. France, the new republic. Oceana. Dobbs Ferry, N. Y. '60.

Aron, Raymond. Great debate: theories of nuclear strategy. Doubleday. Garden City, N. Y. '65.

Aron, Robert. Explanation of de Gaulle. Harper. New York. '66.

Barnet, R. J. and Raskin, M. G. After twenty years: the decline of NATO and the search for a new policy in Europe. Random House (Vintage Books). New York. '66.

Beloff, Nora. General says no. Penguin. Baltimore. '63.

Brzezinski, Z. K. Alternative to partition—for a broader conception of America's role in Europe. McGraw. New York. '65.

Buchan, Alastair, and Windsor, Philip. Arms and stability in Europe. Praeger. New York. '63.

Camps, Miriam. What kind of Europe? The community since de Gaulle's veto. Oxford. New York. '65.

*Cleveland, H. van B. and Cleveland, J. B. Atlantic alliance: problems and prospects. (Headline Series no 177) Foreign Policy Association. 345 E. 46th St. New York 10017. Je. '66.

Cobban, Alfred. History of modern France: v 3, 1871-1962. Penguin. Baltimore. '65.

Coppock, J. O. Atlantic agricultural unity: is it possible? McGraw. New York. '66.

Cottrell, A. J. and Dougherty, J. E. Politics of the Atlantic alliance. Praeger. New York. '64.

Fisher, S. N. ed. France and the European community. Ohio State University Press. Columbus. '64.

*Foreign Policy Association. Great decisions 1966. The Association. 345 E. 46th St. New York 10017. '66.

    Reprinted in this book: Fact Sheet no 3. Western Europe and the United States —end of the Atlantic alliance? p 29-33; Strategic debate. p 34-5.

*Foreign Policy Association. Great decisions 1967. The Association. 345 E. 46th St. New York 10017. '67.

> *Reprinted in this book:* Fact Sheet no 7. NATO in crisis—will the Atlantic alliance survive? p 74-6.

Funk, A. L. Charles de Gaulle: the crucial years. 1943-1944. University of Oklahoma Press. Norman. '59.

Furniss, E. S. Jr. De Gaulle and the French army. Twentieth Century Fund. New York. '64.

Furniss, E. S. Jr. France, troubled ally. Praeger. New York. '60.

*Furniss, E. S. Jr. France under de Gaulle. (Headline Series no 139) Foreign Policy Association. 345 E. 46th St. New York 10017. Ja. '60.

Gaulle, Charles de. Edge of the sword; tr. from the French by Gerard Hopkins. Criterion Bks. '60.

*Gaulle, Charles de. Major addresses, statements and press conferences of General Charles de Gaulle—May 19, 1958-January 31, 1964. French Embassy. 972 5th Ave. New York 10021. '64.

> *Reprinted in this book:* Address by President Charles de Gaulle on French, African and Algerian realities. p 79-81; President de Gaulle's press conference, January 31, 1964. p 250-2.

Gaulle, Charles de. War memoirs of Charles de Gaulle. Simon and Schuster. New York. 3 v.

> V 1: Call to honor, 1940-1942. '55; v 2: Unity, 1942-1944. '59; v 3: Salvation, 1944-1946. '60.

Godfrey, E. D. Government of France. Crowell. New York. '63.

Guérard, Albert. France: a modern history. University of Michigan Press. Ann Arbor. '59.

Haines, C. G. ed. European integration. Johns Hopkins Press. Baltimore. '57.

Hoffmann, Stanley, and others. In search of France. Harvard University Press. Cambridge, Mass. '63.

Kelly, G. A. Lost soldiers: the French army and empire in crisis, 1947-1962. M.I.T. Press. Cambridge, Mass. '65.

Kissinger, H. A. Troubled partnership: a re-appraisal of the Atlantic alliance. Doubleday. Garden City, N. Y. '66.

Kleiman, Robert. Atlantic crisis: American diplomacy confronts a resurgent Europe. Norton. New York. '64.

Kulski, W. W. De Gaulle and the world: the foreign policy of the fifth French republic. Syracuse University Press. Syracuse, N. Y. '66.

Lacouture, Jean. De Gaulle. New American Library. New York. '66.

Lichtheim, George. Marxism in modern France. Columbia University Press. New York. '66.

Lüthy, Herbert. France against herself. Praeger. New York. '55.

Macridis, R. C. ed. De Gaulle: implacable ally. Harper. New York. '66.

Mengin, Robert. No laurels for de Gaulle: an appraisal of the London years. Farrar. New York. '66.

Micaud, C. A. Communism and the French left. Praeger. New York. '63.

Pickles, Dorothy. Fifth French republic: institutions and politics. Praeger. New York. '66.

Pinder, John. Europe against de Gaulle. Praeger. New York. '63.

Schoenbrun, David. Three lives of Charles de Gaulle. Atheneum. New York. '66.

Spears, Sir Edward. Two men who saved France: Pétain and de Gaulle. Stein & Day. New York. '66.

Stanley, T. W. NATO in transition: the future of the Atlantic alliance. Praeger. New York. '65.

Steel, Ronald. End of alliance: America and the future of Europe. Viking. New York. '64.

Strausz-Hupé, Robert, and others. Building the Atlantic world. Harper. New York. '63.

Sulzberger, C. L. The test: de Gaulle and Algeria. Harcourt. New York. '62.

Tournoux, J.-R. Sons of France; Pétain and de Gaulle. Viking. New York. '66.

*United States. Congress. Senate. Committee on Government Operations. Atlantic alliance: allied comment. Supt. of Docs. Washington, D.C. 20402. '66.

   Reprinted in this book: President Charles de Gaulle's press conferences (Excerpts): Third press conference, September 5, 1960. p 35-6; Seventh press conference, January 14, 1963: Common market. p 38-40; President de Gaulle's press conference, September 9, 1965. p 50-2.

Viansson-Ponté, Pierre. King and his court. Houghton. Boston. '64.

Wahl, Nicholas. Fifth Republic: France's new political system. Random House. New York. '59.

Werth, Alexander. De Gaulle; a political biography. Simon and Schuster. New York. '66.

White, D. S. Seeds of discord: de Gaulle, Free France and the allies. Syracuse University Press. Syracuse, N. Y. '64.

PERIODICALS

America. 108:218. F. 16, '63. Future of Europe.

America. 108:628. My. 4, '63. General de Gaulle: pro and con.

America. 110:184-5. F. 8, '64. Gaullist grand design.

America. 113:308. S. 25, '65. De Gaulle's Europe.

America. 114:72-4. Ja. 15, '66. What de Gaulle's re-election means. Robert Bosc.

Annals of the American Academy of Political and Social Science. 351:15-23. Ja. '64. Gaullist revolt against the Anglo-Saxons. C. V. Crabb, Jr.

Atlantic. 212:65-71. Ag. '63. Road to Moscow: de Gaulle and the Kremlin. Curtis Cate.

Atlantic. 215:38+. Ap. '65. Atlantic report.

Atlantic. 215:49-54. Je. '65. On dealing with de Gaulle. J. M. Gavin.

Atlantic. 216:6+. Ag. '65. Atlantic report.

Atlantic. 216:14+. O. '65. Atlantic report.

Atlantic. 217:24+. My. '66. Atlantic report: de Gaulle and NATO.

Atlantic Community Quarterly. 1:541-55. Winter '63-'64. Raison d'être of French defense policy. P. M. Gallois.

Atlantic Community Quarterly. 2:31-4. Spring '64. Wishing to be nothing but French. André Walter.

Atlantic Community Quarterly. 2:45-52. Spring '64. De Gaulle: prophet for Europe or disturber of the peace. Robert Strausz-Hupé.

Atlantic Community Quarterly. 3:155-8, 164-5. Summer '65. Long live France [with reply]. Charles de Gaulle.

Atlantic Community Quarterly. 3:326-31. Fall '65. France: the real Europe. Georges Pompidou.

Atlantic Community Quarterly. 3:479-85. Winter '65-'66. Jean-Charles Snoy.

Atlantic Community Quarterly. 4:17-24. Spring '66. Europe: decision or drift. Dean Acheson.

Atlas. 10:144-7. S. '65. France's road to grandeur. Roy Battersby.

Aviation Week. 81:31. N. 23, '64. France earmarks $5.4 billion for nuclear force development.

Bulletin of the Atomic Scientists. 20:27-9. O. '64. Letter from France; the technocratic age. Bertrand de Jouvenel.

Business Week. p 82-3+. Ja. 26, '63. Can de Gaulle shape Europe to his mold?

Business Week. p 34+. F. 23, '63. France's nuclear sword; nuclear-armed supersonic bombers.

Business Week. p 23-4. Ja. 11, '64. De Gaulle pushes global ambitions.

Business Week. p 52. Mr. 6, '65. Growing rift in French economy.

Business Week. p 45. Ap. 3, '65. De Gaulle rings Kremlin bells.

Business Week. p 36+. Ja. 22, '66. France keeps pressure on Common Market; demand for veto on key issues.

Business Week. p 44+. My. 14, '66. Now de Gaulle likes those Yankee dollars.

Business Week. p 40-1. Je. 11, '66. NATO seeks a new defense line; France determined to quit, but other members want to keep it going.

Business Week. p 128+. S. 10, '66. Special report.

Catholic World. 198:332-4. Mr. '64. De Gaulle's bid to Red China. J. B. Sheerin.

Christian Century. 82:300-3. Mr. 10, '65. Anti-Americanism, French style. E. A. Smith.

*Christian Science Monitor. p 1. Jl. 5, '66. Individualism grows younger. Carlyle Morgan.

*Christian Science Monitor. p 1+. Jl. 25, '66. French cautious on red coalition. Carlyle Morgan.

Commonweal. 77:613-16. Mr. 8, '63. Politics of glory. Michael Harrington.

Commonweal. 80:141-3. Ap. 24, '64. De Gaulle on Vietnam. Ronald Steel.

Commonweal. 83:554-6. F. 11, '66. Suspense in France; de Gaulle muddles through. Stanley Hoffmann.

Commonweal. 84:431. Jl. 8, '66. De Gaulle in the Urals.

Commonweal. 84:570-1. S. 16, '66. U.S. and France. Peter Steinfels.

Current History. 47:332-8+. D. '64. France of Charles de Gaulle. E. W. Fox.

*Current History. 50:193-237+. Ap. '66. France today; symposium.

   Reprinted in this book: New France: changes in French society and culture. Henri Peyre. p 193-200+; French community—does it exist? p 214-20+. Brian Weinstein.

Department of State Bulletin. 52:180-7. F. 8, '65. United States, France, and NATO: a comparison of two approaches; address, January 21, 1965. D. H. Popper.

Department of State Bulletin. 54:617-18. Ap. 18, '66. United States and France exchange views on Atlantic alliance; texts of aides mémoires of March 25, 1966 and March 10, 1966.

*East Europe. 15:2-8. N. '66. De Gaulle's European strategy. James Edwards.

Economist. 214:105-6. Ja. 9, '65. What is Gaullism? life force in power.

Economist. 216:13-14. Jl. 3, '65. After the General.

Economist. 216:109-11. Jl. 10, '65. War for Europe.

Economist. 218:983-4. Mr. 12, '66. Bomb at the heart of NATO.

Foreign Affairs. 41:621-37. Jl. '63. Partners and allies. Alastair Buchan.

Foreign Affairs. 42:546-58. Jl. '64. French people and de Gaulle. Michel Gordey.

Foreign Affairs. 43:487-500. Ap. '65. Which way Europe? J. H. Huizinga.

*Foreign Affairs. 43:561-73. Jl. '65. De Gaulle: pose and policy. Herbert Lüthy.

Foreign Affairs. 44:26-36. O. '65. France and Germany: divergent outlooks. Alfred Grosser.

Foreign Affairs. 44:434-45. Ap. '66. De Gaulle and after. Gaston Defferre.

Foreign Affairs. 44:518-26. Ap. '66. Roosevelt as a friend of France. J. M. Haight.

Foreign Affairs. 45:58-76. O. '66. What is French policy? André Fontaine.

Fortune. 72:126-31+. Ag. '65. Nationalism threatens U.S. investment. R. A. Smith.

Harper's Magazine. 230:69-70+. Mr. '65. Illusionist: why we misread de Gaulle. H. A. Kissinger.

Harper's Magazine. 230:60-5. My. '65. Barges on the Seine. Charles Frankel.

Harper's Magazine. 232:114-17. Ap. '66. Four books on de Gaulle and the future of Europe. J. M. Gavin.

Holiday. 34:62-7. N. '63. Down the Seine. V. S. Pritchett.

International Affairs. 39:198-213. Ap. '63. General de Gaulle and the foreign policy of the Fifth Republic. Alfred Grosser.

International Affairs. 41:11-21. Ja. '65. General de Gaulle and the Anglo-Saxons. David Thompson.

International Affairs. 41:650-62. O. '65. Political principles of General de Gaulle. Douglas Johnson.

International Affairs. 42:410-20. Jl. '66. Making sense of de Gaulle. William Pickles.

International Affairs. 42:421-31. Jl. '66. French nuclear force: a strategic and political evaluation. R. J. Lieber.

International Organization. 18:1-28. Winter '64. De Gaulle, Europe and the Atlantic alliance. Stanley Hoffmann.

Life. 61:18-25. Jl. 8, '66. De Gaulle sets forth to change the face of Europe; with report by C. J. V. Murphy.

Look. 28:38-42+. My. 19, '64. What de Gaulle really wants. Michel Gordey.

Nation. 198:157. F. 17, '64. De Gaulle and Asia.

Nation. 198:195-7. F. 24, '64. De Gaulle's world view. Alexander Werth.

*Nation. 200:99-102. F. 1, '65. Paris-Peking trade; Marianne & the dragon. J. S. Prybyla.

Nation. 200:237, 239-42. Mr. 8, '65. De Gaulle on Vietnam; way out of the jungle; with editorial comment. Alexander Werth.

Nation. 202:200-4. F. 21, '66. De Gaulle and l'affaire; Ben Barka scandal. Alexander Werth.

Nation. 202:350-2. Mr. 28, '66. Ben Barka is dead. Alexander Werth.

Nation. 202:368-70. Mr. 28, '66. Saint Charles. J. J. Kaplow.

National Review. 12:439-42+. Je. 19, '62. De Gaulle's France on the road to neutralism; tr. by James Burnham. Jacques Soustelle.
 Discussion. 14:171-2. F. 26, '63.

National Review. 14:97. F. 12, '63. Crystallization of Gaullism.

National Review. 17:138-40. F. 23, '65. De Gaulle's new triad.

National Review. 17:362. My. 4, '65. Paris-Moscow axis. James Burnham.

*National Review. 18:63-5. Ja. 25, '66. Death of Gaullism. W. S. Schlamm.

National Review. 18:353+. Ap. 19, '66. Oh hateful love, oh loving hate. James Burnham.

National Review. 18:576. Je. 14, '66. NATO trouble: immaturity. E. M. von Kuehnelt-Leddihn.

National Review. 18:916. S. 20, '66. De Gaulle on the loose.

New Leader. 49:12-15. My. 23, '66. Ben Barka fester. Ray Alan.

New Republic. 148:8-9. F. 16, '63. What of the grand design? Raymond Aron.

New Republic. 150:16-18. F. 22, '64. He may be right about China but wrong about Europe. L. J. Halle.

New Republic. 152:10-11. F. 20, '65. Leader of Europe and arbiter between blocs. Jean Daniel.

New Republic. 154:11-12. F. 26, '66. France and the five; de Gaulle's seven-month boycott. Richard Mooney.

*New Republic. 154:19-21. Mr. 12, '66. General de Gaulle and Vietnam. Jean Lacouture.

*New Republic. 154:10-11. Ap. 9, '66. De Gaulle's moves against NATO have a long history: ami, go home. Philip Ben.

New Republic. 154:10. Ap. 30, '66. Sense of insecurity in West Germany: why French troops are wanted. Philip Ben.

New Republic. 154:15-16. My. 7, '66. Empty French chair in Geneva; the force de frappe. Andreas Freund.

New Republic. 154:13-14. Je. 18, '66. De Gaulle's mission to Moscow. Philip Ben.

New Statesman. 71:112-13. Ja. 28, '66. Behind the Ben Barka affair. Olivier Todd.

New Statesman. 71:365-6. Mr. 18, '66. De Gaulle and Nato. Olivier Todd.

New York Times. p 13. Ag. 15, '66. U.S. and de Gaulle. Drew Middleton.

*New York Times. p E 3. O. 9, '66. At home, de Gaulle stands tall. R. E. Mooney.

*New York Times. p 8. O. 29, '66. Excerpts from President de Gaulle's remarks at his news conference.

New York Times. p 14. N. 11, '66. De Gaulle, doubtful of Britain's seriousness, remains cool to admitting her to bloc. R. E. Mooney.

New York Times. p 42. N. 11, '66. Foreign affairs: the view from the Élysée. C. L. Sulzberger.

New York Times Magazine. p 9+. Je. 2, '63. Why de Gaulle cannot win. L. J. Halle.

New York Times Magazine. p 25+. Je. 9, '63. Clues to trans-Atlantic distrust. Michel Gordey.

New York Times Magazine. p 33+. N. 24, '63. France changes, but not Frenchmen. André Maurois.

New York Times Magazine. p 12+. D. 15, '63. After five years, de Gaulle still towers. S. R. Graubard.

New York Times Magazine. p 14-15+. Ja. 12, '64. De Gaulle's non! a year later. L. J. Halle.

New York Times Magazine. p 14+. F. 23, '64. In defense of Charles de Gaulle. Sir J. E. P. Grigg.

New York Times Magazine. p 6+. S. 6, '64. Why the French mistrust us. B. B. Fall.

New York Times Magazine. p 19+. Ja. 10, '65. Case pro and con de Gaulle. Lester Markel.

New York Times Magazine. p 50-1+. N. 14, '65. France transformed; seven years of de Gaulle. Henri Peyre.

New York Times Magazine. p 54-5+. D. 5, '65. Twilight of NATO. Max Frankel.

New York Times Magazine. p 14-15+. My. 29, '66. France is no longer a democracy. François Mitterand.

New Yorker. 41:106+. F. 20; 166+. My. 15; 77-8. Jl. 10; 82-4. Ag. 7; 137+. S. 18; 169-70+. N. 13; 186+. D. 11; 160-1. D. 18, '65; 42:98. Jl. 16; 139-40. S. 10, '66. Letters from Paris. Genêt (Janet Flanner).

Newsweek. 61:11. F. 4, '63. Gaullist explosion. Walter Lippmann.

Newsweek. 61:17-19. F. 11, '63. Alliance: whose grand design?

Newsweek. 63:40-3+. F. 10, '64. France: a return to greatness?

Newsweek. 64:23. N. 30, '64. Gaullism. E. J. Hughes.

Newsweek. 66:40-1. S. 20, '65. And seventy-six trombones.

*Newsweek. 66:43. D. 13, '65. By word and deed, the once and future king.

*Newsweek. 66:44-5. D. 13, '65. Four views on seven years; symposium.

*Newsweek. 66:45-7. D. 13, '65. Who is the real realist?

Newsweek. 67:39. Mr. 28, '66. Doctor de Gaulle; eviction notice to NATO. Kenneth Crawford.

Newsweek. 67:40-1. Ap. 25, '66. De Gaulle is not alone: the view from Europe. Arnaud de Borchgrave.

Newsweek. 67:23. My. 9, '66. Other trouble; de Gaulle's objectives. Walter Lippmann.

Newsweek. 68:34-9. Jl. 4, '66. De Gaulle in Russia: tour de force.

Newsweek. 68:53-4. S. 26, '66. Backyard troubles.

Political Science Quarterly. 78:537-47. D. '63. Economic and political consequences of General de Gaulle. W. R. Burgess.

Political Science Quarterly. 79:335-59. S. '64. Algeria, the army, and the Fifth Republic (1959-61); a scenario of civil-military conflict. G. A. Kelly.

Quarterly Journal of Economics. 79:537-54. N. '65. Whither French planning? B. A. Balassa.

Reader's Digest. 82:101-6. F. '63. Charles de Gaulle, grand master of France.

Reader's Digest. 84:100-4. Ja. '64. What France is out to get. Robert Kleiman.

Reporter. 28:29-32. F. 14, '63. After Brussels. Edmond Taylor.

Reporter. 30:38-41. Ja. 30, '64. Cursing de Gaulle is not a policy. Stanley Hoffmann.

Reporter. 30:24-6. F. 27, '64. France: a third force? Edmond Taylor.

Reporter. 31:41-3. Ag. 13, '64. De Gaulle's Romanian gambit. Edmond Taylor.

Reporter. 32:20-3. F. 25, '65. De Gaulle, Europe, and the dollar. Edmond Taylor.

Reporter. 32:25-8. My. 6, '65. Permissive planning and the French economy. Edmond Taylor.

Reporter. 33:31-2. Jl. 15, '65. Algeria: a rude awakening for the left. Edmond Taylor.

Reporter. 34:37-9. Ja. 13, '66. France's changing policy in Africa. Philippe Decraene.

Reporter. 34:22-8. Mr. 10, '66. Ben Barka affair. Claire Sterling.

Reporter. 34:16-21. Ap. 21, '66. Long NATO crisis. Edmond Taylor.

Reporter. 34:10. Je. 30, '66. Maître de Gaulle; reactions to détente with the Communist powers. Max Ascoli.

Saturday Evening Post. 236:24-8+. N. 23, '63. De Gaulle builds a new France. Don Cook.

Saturday Evening Post. 237:76. F. 29, '64. De Gaulle, Red China and the U.N.

Saturday Evening Post. 238:28-9. D. 4, '65. Find another de Gaulle. Edward Behr.

Saturday Review. 46:44-5. Je. 22, '63. From Napoleon's fall to de Gaulle. Alexander Werth.

Saturday Review. 49:40-1. F. 19, '66. Two sides of a miracle. Alexander Werth.

Saturday Review. 49:29-31. Ag. 6, '66. Gallic paradox. S. K. Padover.

Senior Scholastic. 82:6-9+. Mr. 27, '63. De Gaulle and the future of the Western alliance.

Time. 81:22+. F. 8, '63. New & obscure destination; de Gaulle's veto of Britain's admission to the Common Market.
  Same abridged with title: De Gaulle corners the market. Reader's Digest. 82:65-70. Ap. '63.

Time. 86:108+. O. 1, '65. De Gaulle & business.

Time. 87:33. Ja. 28, '66. L'affaire Ben Barka.

Time. 87:34. F. 25, '66. Duumvirate; M. Debré's plans.

Time. 87:37. Ap. 29, '66. As France sees it.

Time. 87:105. Je. 10, '66. Flight 180 to Shanghai.

Time. 88:20-4+. Jl. 1, '66. Grandest tour; de Gaulle's visit to Russia.

Time. 88:22. Jl. 8, '66. Seeds of disengagement; de Gaulle's visit to Russia.

Travel. 123:52-7. F. '65. Travel's picture portfolio.

U.S. News & World Report. 54:22. Mr. 25, '63. Dealing with de Gaulle; Dean Acheson tells how.

U.S. News & World Report. 56:12. F. 10, '64. Why de Gaulle recognized Red China; summary of news conference.

U.S. News & World Report. 56:70-5. Mr. 16, '64. Why de Gaulle is challenging U.S.; interview. Maurice Couve de Murville.

U.S. News & World Report. 56:64. Je. 29, '64. France's stake in South Asia.

U.S. News & World Report. 57:10. Ag. 3, '64. As de Gaulle sees world issues now; excerpts from news conference, July 23, 1964.

U.S. News & World Report. 57:24-6. D. 28, '64. De Gaulle: just who he is and what's back of him.

U.S. News & World Report. 58:44+. My. 10, '65. Historian looks at de Gaulle: why he acts that way; interview, ed. by F. C. Painton. J. B. Duroselle.

U.S. News & World Report. 58:81. Je. 7, '65. End of the French miracle.

U.S. News & World Report. 58:8. Je. 14, '65. Senator's indictment of de Gaulle; excerpts from address, June 3, 1965. Paul Douglas.

U.S. News & World Report. 59:46-7. Jl. 19, '65. End of Europe's big dream? what de Gaulle's revolt means.

U.S. News & World Report. 59:84-5. Ag. 23, '65. Is de Gaulle killing the Common Market?

U.S. News & World Report. 59:75. O. 18, '65. France without NATO.

U.S. News & World Report. 60:38. Ja. 3, '66. Seven more years of de Gaulle; what to expect.

U.S. News & World Report. 60:36. Mr. 7, '66. What makes de Gaulle act that way?

U.S. News & World Report. 60:26. Mr. 21, '66. Why de Gaulle is so anti-American.

U.S. News & World Report. 60:44-6+. Mr. 21, '66. NATO without France; de Gaulle forces U.S. to showdown in Europe; with analysis by M. S. Johnson.

U.S. News & World Report. 60:36-8. Ap. 4, '66. What U.S. has done for France.

U.S. News & World Report. 60:39-40. Ap. 4, '66. Back of the grandeur: a close look at de Gaulle's France.

U.S. News & World Report. 60:79. Ap. 18, '66. Dean Acheson's word for de Gaulle: nonsense; excerpts from interview. Dean Acheson.

U.S. News & World Report. 60:68. My. 2, '66. French mission to Moscow: what de Gaulle is up to. F. B. Stevens.

U.S. News & World Report. 60:105-6. My. 23, '66. Advice to U.S. on blackmail.

U.S. News & World Report. 60:39-41. Je. 20, '66. Europe's new mood: its meaning for U.S.

U.S. News & World Report. 60:42-3. Je. 20, '66. De Gaulle, the U.S. and Russia: a look at the trends; interview, ed. by F. C. Painton. Alfred Grosser.

U.S. News & World Report. 61:26-7. Jl. 4, '66. De Gaulle in Moscow: what he did, what it means; with report by F. B. Stevens.

*U.S. News & World Report. 61:46+. Jl. 18, '66. Now that France is out of NATO.

U.S. News & World Report. 61:46. S. 19, '66. De Gaulle: no nation has friends, only interests.

Vital Speeches of the Day. 29:230-5. F. 1, '63. Political evolution of Europe; news conference, January 14, 1963. Charles de Gaulle.

Vital Speeches of the Day. 30:55-7. N. 1, '63. Détente and French policy; address, October 22, 1963. H. Alphand.

*Vital Speeches of the Day. 30:75-8. N. 15, '63. France and the Western alliance: actual cooperation is needed; address, October 29, 1963. J. W. Fulbright.
    Summary. U.S. News & World Report. 55:26. N. 11, '63.

Vital Speeches of the Day. 30:197-8. Ja. 15, '64. Future of France; address, December 31, 1963. Charles de Gaulle.

Vital Speeches of the Day. 30:487-90. Je. 1, '64. Nationalism; strength of France; address, April 28, 1964. Maurice Couve de Murville.

Vital Speeches of the Day. 31:101-5. D. 1, '64. French foreign policy; address, November 3, 1964. Maurice Couve de Murville.

Vital Speeches of the Day. 31:212-13. Ja. 15, '65. France 1965; address, December 31, 1964. Charles de Gaulle.

Vital Speeches of the Day. 31:514-15. Je. 15, '65. Independence of France; address, April 27, 1965. Charles de Gaulle.

Vital Speeches of the Day. 31:617-19. Ag. 1, '65. Policy of France; independence of Europe; address, June 17, 1965. Georges Pompidou.

*Vital Speeches of the Day. 32:589-90. Jl. 15, '66. French and Russian cooperation, a European problem; address delivered in Moscow, June 23, 1966. Charles de Gaulle.

*Wall Street Journal. p 1+. Ag. 30, '66. France & Far East: de Gaulle spurs effort to win new influence in old Asian colonies. Robert Keatley.

World Today. 21:112-19. Mr. '65. Gaullist foreign policy. Geoffrey Warner.

World Today. 22:1-13. Ja. '66. General de Gaulle's Europe and Jean Monnet's Europe. J. B. Duroselle.

Yale Review. 55:488-99. Summer '66. Restoration Europe and world politics. Robert Strausz-Hupé.

Yale Review. 55:500-20. Summer '66. De Gaulle and the New France. P. J. Larmour.

DATE DUE

MAY 2 '68			
MAY 8 '68			
MAR 2 0 '69			
APR 17 '69			
MAR 5 '70			
MAR 24 '70			
APR 7 '70			
APR 22 '70			
MAY 5 '70			
MAR 16 '71			
MAY 3 '72			
MAY 7 '75			
FE 21 77			
MY 4 '77			
GAYLORD			PRINTED IN U.S.A.